POSTCARD HISTORY SERIES

Yellowstone National Park

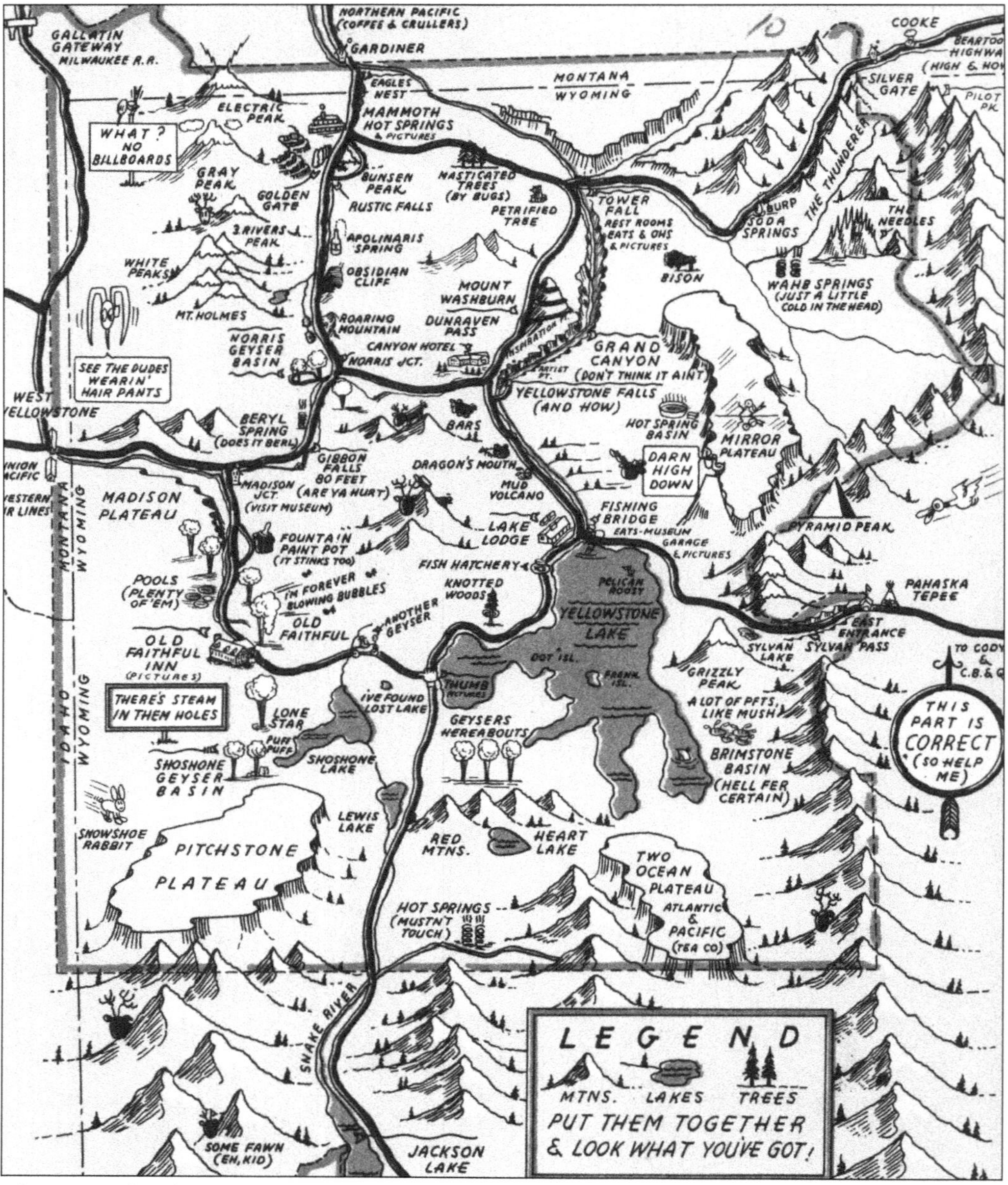

This map of Yellowstone National Park, taken from an oversized postcard printed about 1940, shows the familiar figure-eight roadway loop that skirts most of the park's famous attractions. This book takes the reader on "a grand tour of Yellowstone," starting at Gardiner, the northern entrance. The five gateways to the park, including West Yellowstone, are featured in the last chapter.

ON THE FRONT COVER: Old Faithful Geyser and Old Faithful Inn are seen here about 1910.

ON THE BACK COVER: In 1907, feeding a bear a la carte was commonplace. The practice ceased in the 1930s.

POSTCARD HISTORY SERIES

Yellowstone National Park

Jill Bullock

ARCADIA
PUBLISHING

ISBN 978-0-7385-7503-2

Published by Arcadia Publishing
Charleston, South Carolina

Library of Congress Control Number: 2010941973

For all general information contact Arcadia Publishing at:
Telephone 843-853-2070
Fax 843-853-0044
E-mail sales@arcadiapublishing.com
For customer service and orders:
Toll-Free 1-888-313-2665

Visit us on the Internet at www.arcadiapublishing.com

This book is dedicated to all the early photographers and publishers who strove to provide the public and their friends with the images that are so loved today by collectors and historians. Thanks to their early work and efforts, history was preserved. Today, these eye-candy views bring the past alive for all to enjoy. Many early postcards used in this book are actually photographs developed on postcard-stock paper. These are known as real-photo postcards among collectors in the hobby. A common abbreviation for real-photo postcard is RPPC, and the acronym is used throughout the text of this book.

Contents

Acknowledgments		6
Introduction		7
1.	Through the Arch to Mammoth	9
2.	By Horse to Norris	29
3.	Norris, Fountain, and Lower Basin Features	43
4.	Old Faithful and the Upper Geyser Basin	57
5.	Yellowstone Lake and Its Sights	73
6.	From Canyon to the Valleys and Tower Falls	93
7.	Gateways to Wonderland	115
Bibliography		127

ACKNOWLEDGMENTS

A special thanks to these Yellowstone Park postcard collectors who shared their images and/or expertise in order to significantly enhance this book: Michael H. Francis of Billings; Kathleen M. Burke of Billings; Ron Tobias of Bozeman; Jack and Susan Davis of Bozeman; Ferris Jackson of Livingston; Tal and Val Scott of Nixa, Missouri; Judy and Andy DeBoer of Muskegon, Michigan; Hal Ottaway of Wichita, Kansas; Larry and Thea Lancaster of Oklahoma, Richard Saunders of Tennessee; and J. Michael Bodell of California.

Special thanks go to the staff at Arcadia Publishing for their expertise and technical assistance, and, finally, to Tom Mulvaney, for his unconditional backing and support; without him, this book would never have been possible.

Unless otherwise noted, all images appear courtesy of the author and Tom Mulvaney.

Introduction

Yellowstone. The name conjures up images in the minds of people all over the world: geysers and Old Faithful, great buffalo and bears, canyons, waterfalls, and rustic inns, for Yellowstone National Park has been a fabled destination since its first discovery. The human history of the park begins at least 11,000 years ago, when aboriginal Americans first began to hunt and fish in the region. Over 1,000 archeological sites have been discovered in the area. When white explorers first entered the region in the first decade of the 1800s, their accounts of "fire and brimstone," boiling mud, petrified trees, and steaming rivers were dismissed as delusional ramblings. Today, it is known that half the geothermal features and two-thirds of the world's geysers are concentrated in Yellowstone.

Ferdinand V. Hayden, an enthusiastic advocate, was but one to envision the creation of a park in the Yellowstone region. After an expedition of exploration, he compiled a comprehensive report on Yellowstone for Congress that helped to convince members to withdraw this region from public auction. Hayden concluded that if Congress failed to pass a bill to protect the area, "the vandals who are now waiting to enter into this wonder-land, will in a single season despoil, beyond recovery, these remarkable curiosities, which have requited all the cunning skill of nature thousands of years to prepare." He envisioned "setting aside the area as a pleasure ground for the benefit and enjoyment of the people" and warned that there were those who would come and "make merchandise of these beautiful specimens."

In an unprecedented act, Congress passed the Yellowstone Park bill which was signed into law on March 1, 1872, by Pres. Ulysses S. Grant and made the park the world's first truly national park. It soon became evident that while Congress had created this national park, it had not made any provision for an authority to oversee it, and the need to protect the park was quickly recognized. Ongoing poaching and destruction of natural resources continued unabated until men from the 1st US Cavalry, under Capt. Moses Harris, arrived at Mammoth in 1886 and built Camp Sheridan. In 1891, this became Fort Yellowstone.

Still, park wildlife was routinely killed; livestock overgrazed park meadows; ancient forests were still under threat; tourists carved their names on rocks and trees, and young ladies were observed using their hairpins to scrawl their names in the bottoms of shallow pools. Protecting the park was dangerous work. In the frigid winter season, cavalrymen on skis patrolled for poachers. Conditions were often treacherous; soldiers died in avalanches and snowstorms, or were killed by poachers. Protecting the park was a mammoth task. As America moved into a new century, a new word, *conservation*, crept into the nation's vocabulary. A growing awareness surfaced that the nation's unrelenting rush to conquer and tame the land had come at a terrible cost. Forests had been devastated, and entire species of animals had been ravaged—all in the name of progress.

A new president, Theodore Roosevelt, became conservation's greatest advocate and turned the word into a movement. When he made his second visit to Yellowstone in 1903, he delighted in seeing so many animals, especially since the increase in game animals could be attributed to the wildlife protection bill that he, along with George Bird Grinnell and John F. Lacey, had worked so hard to pass. Over time, with the funding and manpower necessary to keep a diligent watch, the Army developed its own policy regulations that permitted public access while protecting park wildlife and natural resources.

The grand tour, the idea of traveling for the sake of curiosity and learning, was an idea that began in Europe in the 17th century, the argument for it being that knowledge comes entirely from the external senses. Travel, therefore, was necessary for one to develop the mind and expand knowledge. Yellowstone became America's unique, own "grand tour," and the experience of early tourists in the park was quite unlike that of today's visitors. Yellowstone at first was not a park for all people due to the expense of reaching it, but with the coming of the railroad to Gardiner, Montana, in 1883, this began to change. Yellowstone was on its way to becoming an enjoyable vacation destination for many, although there remained a few inconveniences.

Stagecoach travel could be bumpy and dusty, although the scenery more than compensated. The coaches frequently had to be unloaded at steep grades, giving the passengers an opportunity to stretch their legs and breathe in the cool air while following the vehicles uphill. Being the Wild West, there were a few holdups with victims often entranced with their robbers. A robbery could be an added bit of excitement to an already enjoyable tour. As one tourist remarked, "We think we got off cheap and would not sell our experience, if we could, for what it cost us."

Typically, an early tour of Yellowstone began when tourists descending from the train outfitted in their finery were given linen dusters, boarded onto large stagecoaches, and then taken up the scenic Gardner River canyon to Mammoth Hot Springs. At Mammoth, one could tour the terraces or have the opportunity to bathe in the hot springs, one of the greatest attractions. In a day when a hot bath was a luxury and people were less sophisticated about their medical needs, hot mineral baths were popularly believed to have curative powers—not to mention providing the simple pleasure of soaking in hot water.

For the next few days, the tourists bounced along in horse-drawn coaches called "Yellowstone wagons." They were entertained by the colorful profanity of the stage drivers, who urged their horses over the dusty roads of the Grand Loop. The stagecoaches were spaced 500 yards apart to less lessen the effects of dust that author Rudyard Kipling labeled "dense as a fog." During the halts at important natural features, the drivers amazed their passengers with exceedingly imaginary explanations of the natural history. Days were devoted to visiting the geysers, thermal pools, and fumaroles where tourists would peer down holes in the ground, taking their chances that a geyser was not about to erupt with them on the spot. They washed pieces of linen in Handkerchief Pool, which quickly turned the cloth white as snow. Geysers were "soaped," a practice of pouring laundry soap down its mouth in the belief that it would hasten eruptions.

By 1900, people were enjoying the nightly spectacle of bears being fed hotel garbage, and some even helped with the feeding, few worrying about the effect on the bears or the danger to themselves. Boats offered peaceful tours of Yellowstone Lake, while back at Mammoth, wildlife could be closely observed at the game corral. In contrast to elaborate hotels, rustic tent camps provided simple but comfortable accommodations among the trees at lesser cost for those so inclined.

The National Park Service was created in 1916, and many of the management principles developed by the US Army at Yellowstone were adopted by the new agency when it took control on October 31, 1918. The stated function of the National Park Service is "to promote and regulate the use of the . . . national parks . . . which purpose is to conserve the scenery and the natural and historic objects and the wild life therein and to provide for the enjoyment of the same in such manner and by such means as will leave them unimpaired for the enjoyment of future generations." As from the beginning, Yellowstone remains a work in progress as its keepers struggle to determine just how to manage the parklands and what should and should not be allowed.

By 1915, an estimated 1,000 automobiles per year entered the park, resulting in conflicts with horse-drawn transportation. Horses were relegated first to the backcountry and then prohibited, while many of the tent camps, hotels, lunch stations, and eventually all but one of the transportation companies disappeared. These were replaced by paved roads, parking areas convenient to scenic attractions, service stations, and public campgrounds to accommodate motorized visitors. Between 1933 and 1941, the Civilian Conservation Corps built the majority of the early visitor centers, campgrounds and the current system of park roads. Today, over three million people a year enter its portals, and Yellowstone has become a truly *national* park, accessible to all.

One

Through the Arch to Mammoth

On the main street of Gardiner, Montana, four horses pull a stagecoach holding a driver and passengers in this 1909 RPPC. The stage has just passed both a souvenir store advertising "Park Views" and the Wylie Hotel. A message penned on the reverse side says, "Dear Beulah. This is how the bunch looks when we go through the Park though we won't be quite so thick on one seat." Gardiner has served as Yellowstone's northern entrance town from the earliest days.

Pres. Theodore Roosevelt, for whom the Roosevelt Arch at Gardiner is named, poses for this 1903 RPPC at Fort Yellowstone. On his 1903 tour of Yellowstone Park, Roosevelt dedicated the arch inscribed with the quote "For the Benefit and Enjoyment of the People" by laying the cornerstone. The cornerstone covered a time capsule that contains a Bible, a picture of Roosevelt, local newspapers, and other items.

A Northern Pacific Railway train bringing tourists to the park's northern entrance is shown arriving at the depot in Gardiner. Gardiner was the first major entrance to Yellowstone. The large building, center background, is the W.A. Hall store, which, according to the large sign in front, "Sells Everything." This card, postmarked from Gardiner in 1908, was published on behalf of the Shaw & Powell Camping Company.

On July 4, 1887, masked amateur road agents Charlie Higgenbotham and William James held up the Bighorn, Yellowstone's first six-horse stage, at Eagle Nest Rock in Gardiner Canyon. The thieves relieved passengers of $16 cash. The two, later overheard in a saloon talking about the robbery, ended up in the Montana Territorial Prison. Stagecoach robberies in Yellowstone did occur in the early days, and the horseback rider at the right may be an armed guard.

In 1886, control over the park was delegated to the US Army, as civilian authorities were unable to protect the park's natural features or halt the poaching of wildlife. Fort Yellowstone, near the Mammoth Hot Springs Hotel, was the site of one US Army tent campsite, as shown here in 1908. Fort Yellowstone served as the administrative headquarters for the Army base in Yellowstone Park.

Antelope graze in an alfalfa field near the entrance to the park at Gardiner in this c. 1910 view. The Roosevelt Arch is visible in the right background. At nearby Mammoth, six miles into the park, the meadows were used to grow alfalfa hay that was used to feed the elk, buffalo, and other wildlife during the long, cold winter months.

In 1902, only a few hundred buffalo remained in the United States, with only 23 surviving in the wild. The buffalo was facing extinction, and in response to a public outcry, Congress purchased a small herd that was at first kept in an enclosure near Mammoth. Wild calves captured in the spring were raised for interbreeding, and the animals thrived under the close watch of their keepers.

Here, elk and deer are taking part in the "free lunch" program at the park in 1923. Text printed on the back includes the following: "There are thousands of these stately animals in the Park. It is a natural wonder that their great antlers can be grown to maturity in a few months to be discarded and regrown each year. Elk and deer frequently graze together by the roadside."

Captioned "Unloading Elk from Yellowstone Park Train, Livingston, Mont. Nov – 4 – 1919," this RPPC includes this message on the back: "Livingston, Mont. This is the way they are slaughtering Elk near Yellowstone Park now. 130 were brought here yesterday." This card was postmarked from Livingston on Nov. 9, 1919, and mailed to Chicago. From a postcard history standpoint, this card documents the speed by which photographers could produce real-photo postcards and make them available to the public.

Published for the Northern Pacific Railway, this card is captioned "Mammoth Hotel and Stages, Yellowstone Park." The message penned on the back includes the following passage: "We arrived here this a.m. Got washed and had lunch. Then took a sight seeing drive for a couple of hours and things certainly are wonderful here. You could never imagine them, but quite like the cards." This card was mailed back east to Norristown, Pennsylvania, in 1912.

Liberty Cap is a 37-foot-tall extinct hot spring cone. The unusual formation was created by a hot spring whose plumbing remained open and in one location for a long time. Its internal pressure was sufficient to raise the water to a great height, allowing mineral deposits to build continuously, layer upon layer. Two wooden structures, one in the foreground and one to the right of Liberty Cap, are early bathhouses. When first seen, Liberty Cap was reported as 52 feet in height.

These two rare 1912 RPPC views are captioned, "Birds Eye View – Pool & Sulphur Mt. Yellowstone Park" (above) and "Sulphur Mt. And Hot Spring, Yellowstone Park" (below). At the time, Mammoth was often referred to as Sulphur Mountain. The reservoir dam pictured was built by Hiram Chittenden below Marble Terrace, and it can still be seen today if searched for. Although built as a source of hydroelectric power for Fort Yellowstone, the water was also used for irrigation. The water source was Glen Creek, which was channeled by means of a ditch that ran to this spot from nearly three miles to the south.

The stepped terraces at Mammoth Hot Springs are the result of the largest known carbonate-depositing spring in the world. The area lies along the Morris-Mammoth Earthquake Fault, and this large hill of travertine was created over a period of thousands of years. Groundwater seeps downward and comes into contact with hot gases charged with carbon dioxide rising from a volcanic magma chamber, and a weak carbonic acid solution is created. This hot, acidic solution dissolves great quantities of limestone as it works up through rock layers to the surface hot springs. On being exposed to the air, the carbon dioxide is released from the solution and a solid mineral is reformed and deposited as the travertine that forms the terraces. Over two tons of calcium carbonate flow into Mammoth each day in solution. The terraces are constantly changing shape and color because of minor earthquake activity that shifts spring vents, rendering some areas dry, gray, and lifeless.

This 1880 stereograph image captioned "Pulpit Terraces, Coating Springs" shows a well-dressed man holding a travertine-coated specimen, possibly a horseshoe. Customers brought coins, hairpins, horseshoes, bottles, and other items to be coated with the minerals contained in the water. Coating was usually done on only a few racks at a time, while the older racks were left in place to eventually become totally covered in travertine and a permanent part of the terraces.

Otherworldly beauty can easily be imagined in this 1921 RPPC showing the contours of Angel Terraces. Note the dead trees, which have been overrun by the expanding mineral deposits left by the flowing water that formed these exquisite terraces. Known for these pure white formations from its active periods, Angel Terrace is one of the area's most unpredictable features. Once dry and brittle, it is now showing new signs of awakening thermal activity. (Photograph by H.E. High, Denver, Colorado, 1921.)

Text printed on this card's reverse includes the following: "This geyser is in Mammoth Hot Springs, on a terrace above the Narrow Gauge. It is an oblong mound of deposit twenty feet high and twenty feet in diameter, and is active and brilliantly colored." Orange Spring Mound was formed over the course of thousands of years from a combination of sluggish water movement and small mineral deposits. Its unique streaks of color are created by the presence of algae and microscopic bacteria.

This rare RPPC shows Bath Lake, a once-popular bathing site for Fort Yellowstone soldiers. Early tourists swimming there probably viewed the experience with mixed emotions, for although the warm water was soothing, the skin became encrusted with calcium carbonate to the extent that one's body appeared to be whitewashed. Today, Bath Lake experiences dramatic changes in thermal activity, partially caused by the destruction of fragile formations during its bathtub days. (Courtesy of Francis Historical Collection.)

In the park's early days, a ladder descended down into the Devil's Kitchen, a deep fissure in the rocks. This long, narrow underground chamber passageway was about 75 feet long by 35 feet deep and typical of the hollow area from which springs in the area originate. The walls were warm, and the heat increased as one descended. The ladder was removed in 1939 due to the presence of carbon dioxide fumes.

Cupid's Cave was located at Mammoth Hot Springs, and 100 years ago it was described as "a vapory cavern" with colorful algae growing in it. Today, it is known that the "algae" were in fact a type of bacteria. In the 1930s, the discharge from nearby Cupid Spring became nearly continuous, and the mineral deposits in its flow over time have filled in and sealed the cave.

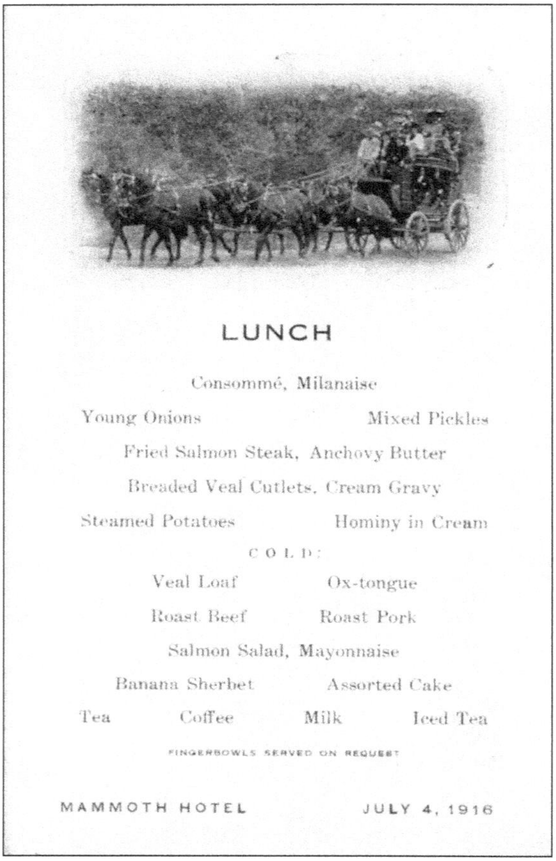
LUNCH

Consommé, Milanaise

Young Onions | Mixed Pickles

Fried Salmon Steak, Anchovy Butter

Breaded Veal Cutlets, Cream Gravy

Steamed Potatoes | Hominy in Cream

COLD:

Veal Loaf | Ox-tongue

Roast Beef | Roast Pork

Salmon Salad, Mayonnaise

Banana Sherbet | Assorted Cake

Tea | Coffee | Milk | Iced Tea

FINGERBOWLS SERVED ON REQUEST

MAMMOTH HOTEL | JULY 4, 1916

The front of the above card (not shown) shows the Mammoth Hot Springs Hotel and is headed "MENU." This card was issued as part of the hotel's celebration of July 4, 1916. When this double-sized card is opened, it reveals the lunch menu for the day shown on the left side. The c. 1916 card below, published by the Northern Pacific Railway, shows the hotel as it appeared in 1913, newly remodeled. The added wing was set at an angle to provide stability, and the roof was also lowered. The railroad did not actually extend to Mammoth but terminated six miles north at Gardiner.

The above image shows the right interior of the double-sized postcard described on the previous page. Two pictures, including one of the Grand Canyon and one of the Lower Falls, are shown along with the day's program of events. The day started with a baseball game between the hotel employees and the soldiers at 9:30 a.m. and was followed by a 48-gun salute at noon. Surrey rides and footraces highlighted the afternoon activities. The postcard below shows an interior view of the Mammoth Hotel lobby at the time.

23206. MAMMOTH CAMP MAIN BUILDING, YELLOWSTONE PARK. HAYNES PHOTO.

Built in 1917 at a cost of $70,000, the Mammoth Lodge was intended to replace the Wylie Camps at Swan Lake Flats and Willow Flats. Its design was formulated on the premise that it was to function as intermediary accommodations falling between those of a hotel and that of a campground. In 1920, a swimming pool was added, and in 1922 and 1923, a main lodge building, laundry, kitchen, offices, and dining room were constructed. This facility included a large complex of cabins. On October 30, 1930, the laundry and boiler room caught fire and burned down without the flames spreading to the lodge. The lodge was abandoned in 1940, and torn down in 1949. The large flag-draped lobby shown below lends credence to the term national park.

23291. MAMMOTH CAMP LOBBY, YELLOWSTONE PARK. HAYNES PHOTO.

The most elaborate and ornamental of the terraces at Mammoth are the Pulpit Terraces. These are a succession of magnificent terraces, 50 feet high, with beautifully colored columnar supports as illustrated here in this c. 1920 RPPC. The Mammoth Lodge can be seen below on the flats of Capitol Hill with the permanent tent camp visible. These canvas tents were characterized as rustic simplicity, having wooden floors, some solid furniture, and nice bedding.

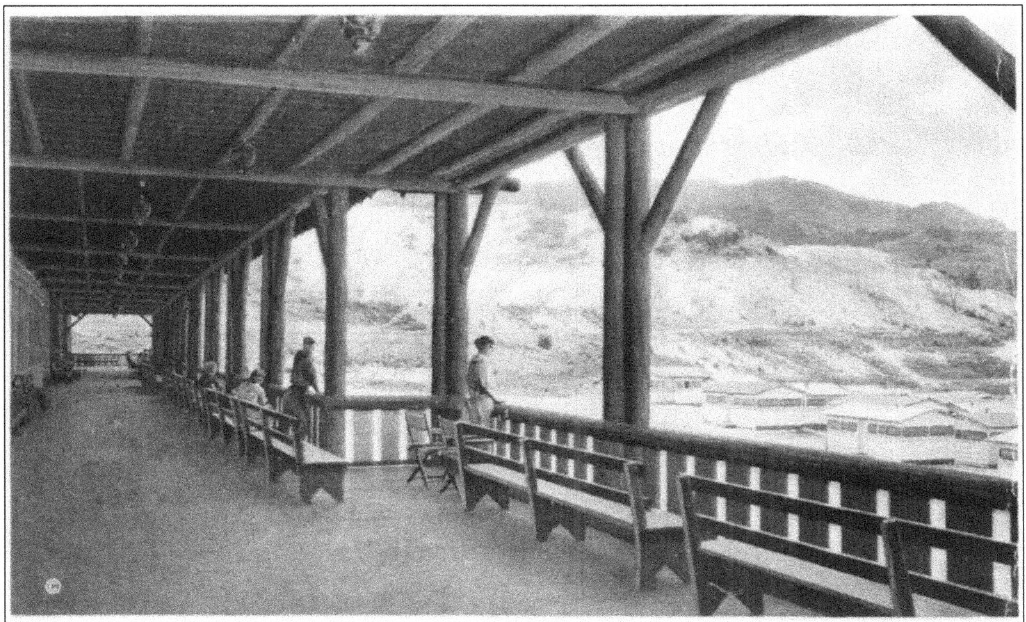

In this view, titled "Jupiter Terrace from Mammoth Camp, Yellowstone Park," visitors stand on the porch of the large central building and look out over the cabins that were built to replace the permanent tents. From here, one sees the valley stretching out to the terraces beyond.

Text printed on the reverse of this card postmarked in 1926 states, "This view shows one of the permanent lodges erected for the comfort of its guests." At that time, a large complex of these cabins was erected between the main lodge and the swimming pool. In the late 1930s, seventy of these cabins were moved to the Roosevelt Lodge area.

This 1910 postcard shows an "Elk Antler Fence," one of the ornamental uses of shed elk antlers. Every year, bulls, some with very impressive antlers, make their way to the Mammoth area to compete for the attention of elk cows during the mating season. At times, they are a threat to people and property. The first Haynes photography studio at Mammoth sat in the middle of the parade grounds, surrounded by an elk antler fence.

The "House of Antlers," as shown in 1936, stood in front of the Headquarters Museum at Mammoth. It was constructed principally of shed wapiti (elk) antlers with the addition of a few from deer and moose. Although in its time one of the most frequently photographed "buildings" in the park, it was removed to discourage tourists from collecting antlers. Mice, squirrels, and other small animals chew on the antlers to get needed minerals.

This Haynes Picture Shop building was constructed at Mammoth in 1929. The upper floor on the right holds the central offices, and the retail space is behind the large windows. A printing plant and a separate warehouse were also in use. This remarkable family's legacy as the "House of Haynes" began in the 1880s, and it shall forever be remembered for its contribution to history in recording much of Yellowstone's and Montana's pasts.

Two 1910 postcards show Fort Yellowstone, the parade grounds, and the hotel at the time when the Army's presence was at its peak with 324 soldiers. It was here in 1886 that the US Cavalry arrived to begin more than 30 years of military presence, first living in temporary frame buildings established at the foot of the terraces. After enduring five cold, harsh winters, it was realized that this was an assignment without end in sight, and Congress appropriated $50,000 for a permanent post in 1890. Completed in 1891, Fort Yellowstone consisted of soldier barracks, officers' quarters, stables, a guardhouse, and administrative headquarters. Built on an old travertine terrace, there was concern that the hollow ground would not support the weight of the buildings. This explains the large fenced-off sinkholes on the parade grounds. When the National Park Service assumed management of the park in 1918, it adopted Fort Yellowstone as its headquarters, and it remains such today.

The above 1955 postcard is captioned on back, "Tourist admiring Deer and Terraces at Mammoth Hot Springs in Yellowstone National Park." The old Mammoth Hotel was torn down in 1936, and a new complex of buildings was constructed as shown in the 1940 RPPC below. The only remnant of the old hotel remaining is the 1913 North Wing. Today, it contains all of the guestrooms in use. A large lobby with lounge, a portico, and offices upstairs in front of the old North Wing were also added. A separate restaurant was built across the road (center left), and it utilized some of the original hotel foundations. Additionally, a building containing a recreation hall, fountain, and café were built behind the hotel.

The 1968 postcard above is captioned on back "Wintertime Bus Tours, in Yellowstone National Park, Wyoming. The scenic excursions operate daily from Mammoth Motor Inn near Yellowstone's north entrance at Gardiner, Montana – The Inn is open year around. Passengers can see an unusual winter wonderland abounding with native wildlife and white landscapes." In 1937–1938, a complex of cabins was erected along the edge of the hill for the ever-growing number of auto tourists. By the 1950s, the hotel became known as the Mammoth Motor Inn. The 1954 postcard below shows the lounge and map room of the present hotel. This room features a huge map of the United States pieced together with a variety of different woods, designed by renowned architect Robert C. Reamer.

Two

By Horse to Norris

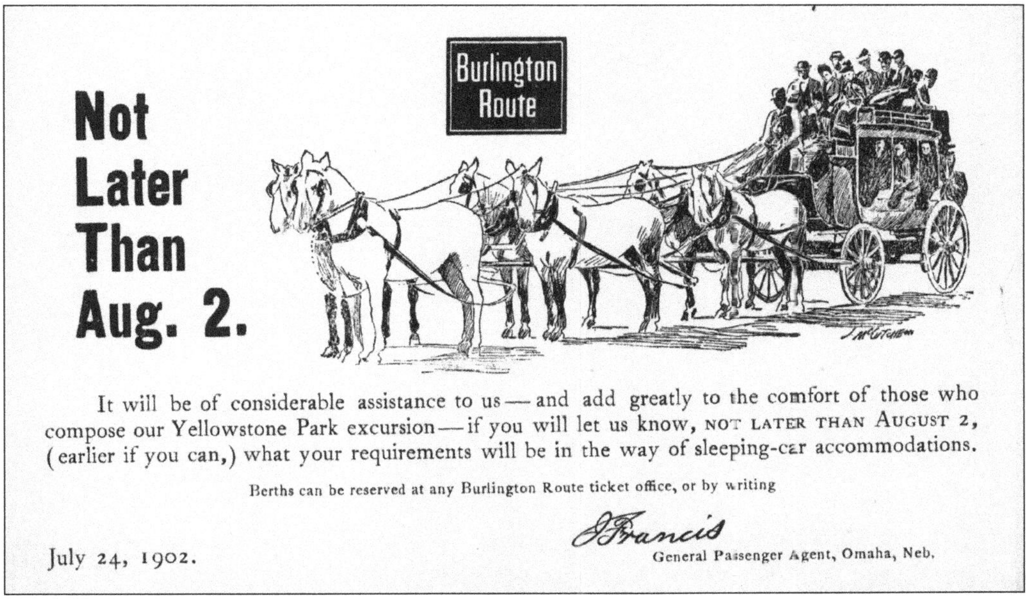

This July 24, 1902, Burlington Railroad advertising postcard shows a six-horse tallyho. These coaches operated exclusively out of Gardiner at the northern entrance of the Park and were used to transport travelers from the Gardiner, Montana, railroad depot to the hotels at Mammoth Hot Springs. This advertisement was printed on the reverse of a US government postal card.

This image, taken from a c. 1902 stereograph, shows a horse-drawn buggy heading south from Mammoth Hot Springs in the direction of Bunsen's Peak. Today, this peak is a popular hiking destination. A relatively short two-mile trail takes hikers to the top of Bunsen Peak, an isolated volcanic cone. This peak rises 1,400 feet above its surroundings and is located three miles south of Mammoth Village.

The Hoodoos are one of the strangest formations of the park. They cover an area of about one square mile. In their midst, the roadway makes an abrupt turn between great blocks of limestone that rise fully 70 feet and to which the name Silver Gate is aptly applied.

WYLIE SERIES No. 3. A WYLIE TWO-COMPARTMENT TENT INTERIOR—YELLOWSTONE PARK. HAYNES-PUB.

The Wylie Camp at Swan Lake Flats was in operation during the years 1906 to 1916. Located just a few miles south of Mammoth Hot Springs, the camp's demise was heralded by the arrival of the automobile into the park. Advertising on the reverse side reads, "I am entering 'Wonderland' today the 'Wylie Way' which means a complete and comfortable camping tour." The tent camps were set up in a permanent manner throughout the traveling season.

WYLIE SERIES No. 2. ONE OF THE EIGHT WYLIE CAMPS—YELLOWSTONE PARK. HAYNES-PUB.

Seeing the park the "Wylie Way" was developed to accommodate tourists who wished travel the park by camping. The Wylie Company developed eight campsites, supplied all needed equipment, and provided two lunch stations. Photographer Harry Shipler took this photograph of the Swan Lake Flats camp. In the winter, the camps were dismantled and hauled to company warehouses at Canyon and Gardiner. This 1910 postcard has a Wylie advertisement on the reverse.

Having two inside seats and a box, this four-horse stagecoach was designed for nine passengers. In 1907, tour information said that if the party numbered from seven to eleven, a coach for the regular tour would be set aside for the party's exclusive use. If there were fewer than seven in the party, they could have a coach to themselves if they paid for unfilled seats.

This 1910 postcard image shows "A Shaw & Powell Camping Wagon" in the park. Shaw & Powell operated portable tent camps, and a cook wagon such as the one shown here accompanied the touring group for meal preparation. The company carried all the needed supplies with them and set up nightly camps in various locations that featured good grass for grazing and adequate water resources.

This 1910 postcard view shows "A Marshall Camping Party, Yellowstone National Park." Like other outfitters of the time, the Marshall Company transported its guests in wagons and coaches around the park to view the major scenic attractions. Tent camping was a much more modest and less expensive way to tour. Perhaps a dusty and tiresome day accounts for the lack of smiles in this group portrait.

"Sagebrushers" were those who traveled in private camping parties and came prepared to camp in the wild. They brought their own equipment, enjoyed the sights, and camped wherever night overtook them. Some lingered all summer long in the mountains, moving on only when their spirits stirred them. These visitors were often looked down upon and were seldom permitted access to the park's restaurants and hotels. Here, they are stopped at the point of a dead animal in the roadway.

The first road through Golden Gate Canyon, built by Lt. Dan Kingman, was so named for the gold-colored lichens growing on its rock walls. The previous route through Snow Pass was steeper, and the Golden Gate, although an engineering challenge, provided a route that was more easily passable. The sign on this bridge of wooden scaffolding advises, "Walk Your Horses." This image is from an 1890 stereograph.

This 1910 RPPC shows a military troop marching on the road near Golden Gate. Officers on horseback are in the lead, as seen in the foreground. This contingent is probably returning to Fort Yellowstone in the Mammoth Hot Springs area, a distance of about five miles from Golden Gate.

A horse-drawn buggy makes its way on the road near Golden Gate, as shown in this 1890 stereograph image. The solitary boulder at the right, the Pillar of Hercules, has been removed and replaced each time the road has been widened and the bridge renovated. It was placed upon its own pillar to rest during a 1933–1934 road construction project.

In 1901, the wooden bridge at Golden Gate was replaced by a one-lane, all-concrete viaduct built by the Army Corps of Engineers in conjunction with the construction of 400 miles of road in the park. The Pillar of Hercules, which still stands today like a sentinel, is visible close to where the road curves out of sight. This 1909 view was published for the Northern Pacific Railway.

The Sheepeater Cliff was named after a band of the Shoshone, the Tukudika, or Sheepeaters, that was the only group of Indians known to have permanently lived in the park. They subsisted on big horn sheep, which were plentiful in the region. They were forced to move elsewhere, but their presence is commemorated in the name of these columnar basalt formations, Sheepeater Cliff.

In 1912, the Shaw & Powell Camping Company was given permission to build a permanent camp at Willow Park, shown in this c. 1916 postcard. Willow Park was located near today's Indian Creek Campground. In 1913, the company was granted a 10-year lease to build camps at six other major locations in the park. By 1916, most construction, which included storerooms, dining rooms, and kitchens, was completed at these sites.

This RPPC image, published in the early 1920s, is captioned "No. 37 – Camp Grounds, Yellowstone Park." The location is not indicated, but this may be another view of the Willow Park Camp run by the Shaw & Powell Camping Company. An automobile is parked in the shade at the right. Created by Amos Shaw and J. D. Powell, Shaw & Powell operated mobile camps throughout the park.

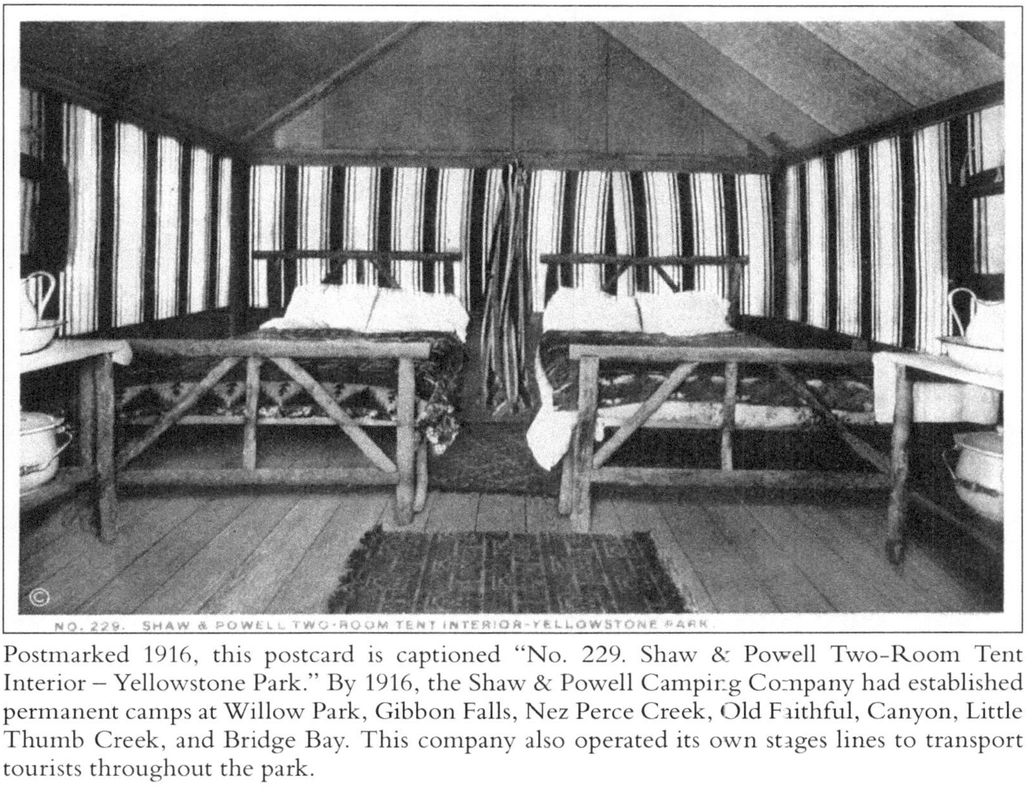

Postmarked 1916, this postcard is captioned "No. 229. Shaw & Powell Two-Room Tent Interior – Yellowstone Park." By 1916, the Shaw & Powell Camping Company had established permanent camps at Willow Park, Gibbon Falls, Nez Perce Creek, Old Faithful, Canyon, Little Thumb Creek, and Bridge Bay. This company also operated its own stages lines to transport tourists throughout the park.

This 1910 RPPC is captioned "Camp Apollinaris Spring" and shows many of the tents set up at this US Army camp. From here, it was about a 10-mile march north to Fort Yellowstone and a nearly similar distance to hike south to the Norris Geyser Basin. This camp was likely in the vicinity of the original Wylie camp that had been established in this area in 1898.

The first fountain at Apollinaris Spring is shown here before it was enlarged in the 1920s. This important mineral water spring supplied water for stagecoach tourists traveling the route between Golden Gate and Norris Basin. The water from the spring reminded early Yellowstone visitors of carbonated water. The paths and the natural well were replaced in 1925 by multiple fountains and an area of stone landscaping for the convenience of visitors.

This famous bear photograph, named Madonna of the Wilds, first appeared in the National Geographic Magazine and in the Yellowstone Park Guide. Jack E. Haynes released this popular image in RPPC format about 1945. The park is prime habitat for both grizzly bears and black bears. Grizzlies are usually seen in the open areas, while black bears are seen along the edges of forests in the Lamar and Hayden Valleys, or among the trees near Mammoth and Tower.

Postmarked 1918, this postcard is captioned "Ranger and Bears, Old Faithful District, Yellowstone Park, Wyo." Park rangers, under the auspices of the National Park Service, became responsible for law enforcement, traffic control, and many other services in Yellowstone about this time. Former president Gerald R. Ford served as a seasonal ranger at Yellowstone in 1936. Today, visitors can check out The Museum of the National Park Ranger, located in Norris Campground. (Courtesy of Kathie Burke.)

The Army camp at Camp Obsidian Creek is shown in this 1910 RPPC view. With Fort Yellowstone in Mammoth serving as a base, troops marched to various parts of Yellowstone to show their presence and maintain authority. This camp was near Obsidian Cliff, about 14 miles south of Fort Yellowstone. The US Army remained in the park for eight more years, leaving for good in 1918 when the National Park Service assumed management.

For centuries, many Indian tribes journeyed to this mountain of black glass for the material which was used to make spear points, knives, and arrowheads. The first white explorers found the area almost impassable, and lore says that they piled timber at the cliffs base and set it afire. When the glass was hot it shattered into fragments when dashed with cold water from the lake at its base. These fragments were then pushed into the lake, making a roadbed.

There is a tall tale allegedly imparted by the old trapper Jim Bridger about Obsidian Cliff, shown above in a 1925 view. It goes that one day, he shot at an elk grazing in a nearby meadow. Not only did it not fall over dead, it was not even spooked, not even after several shots. So he decided to club it to death with his rifle, and as he was running to do so, he ran into a mountain of glass. In addition, this glass mountain was shaped like a lens, and the reflected elk was actually miles away. The c. 1922 view (below) shows the hillside of Roaring Mountain filled with fumaroles, or steam vents, which are the hottest hydrothermal features in the park. These vents contain small amounts of water, and the intense heat converts all the water into steam before it reaches the surface, resulting in a loud hissing sound.

The fringed gentian (*Gentiana elegans*) is shown in this 1925 postcard view published by Jack E. Haynes. In *The Yellowstone National Park—Historical and Descriptive*, Hiram Martin Chittenden shared an experienced collector's description of the fringed gentian as "the characteristic flower of the Park as well as the most beautiful." While this is perhaps too sweeping a claim, the flower is certainly very abundant and of great beauty. It grows in the lower, moist meadows and in the vicinity of the geyser basins. Few flowers display so fine a texture or have such a rich deep blue color, although some white specimens have been observed.

This is a very rare 1910 postcard view advertising a Kodak Stereopticon lecture featuring 60 hand-colored slides of Yellowstone Park: "One hour lecture. Just think of it. A picture every minute." Thankfully, entrepreneurs and photographers such as these made it possible for today's generations to "see our Great National Park as the Kodak saw it" over 100 years ago.

Three

Norris, Fountain, and Lower Basin Features

The Yellowstone Park Hotels made it point to reach out to potential park visitors (and customers). These cards were handed out to guests at the park hotels with requests that they supply "the name and address in the space provided below of any friend whom you think would be interested in literature concerning Yellowstone Park," These cards could be dropped in the hotel mailbox.

In 1901, a new combination lunch station and hotel was built at Norris Geyser Basin, the first geyser basin reached on the Grand Loop trip after leaving Mammoth. Here, tourists could sit on a broad, sheltered veranda and enjoy the sights of the thermal geyser basin below. This was the third hotel to be built at Norris. Although it was small and had only about 25 sleeping rooms, the lodging offered lunch and a comfortable vista.

Publishers of postcards did not always get their captions correct—as in the case with this card. The boiling hot, vivid green Emerald Spring is actually located in the Norris Geyser Basin. It is one of the first sights on the boardwalk trail. A hot spring is a spring that is produced by the emergence of geothermally heated groundwater from the earth's crust. This spring is 27 feet deep.

Today, New Crater Geyser is known as Steamboat Geyser, famous for being the world's tallest geyser, and known to shoot water over 400 feet into the air. Steamboat had been dormant for over 50 years when it came back to life following the 1959 Hebgen earthquake. The lower image, showing Steamboat in the first daylight eruption after its reawakening, was taken by the author, who had spent four days in the basin below, waiting, feeling as if an eruption was imminent. The author was also present at Steamboat when the last eruption occurred on May 23, 2005, being one of the few fortunate people in the world who has witnessed two Steamboat eruptions from the start of the "water phase" on into the "steam phase." Full eruptions are accompanied by a loud roar, and it is not uncommon for boulders to be thrown about. For hours following the rare major water eruptions, which last between 3 and 40 minutes, this magnificent geyser thunders with powerful steam jets. (Below, courtesy of Terri Crawford.)

The sinter, spine covered crater of Echinus Geyser reminds one of a spiny sea urchin, the name deriving from the Greek word for spiny. Until recently this was the largest predictable geyser in the Norris Basin with fountain-type bursts to 75 feet. Most geysers in the world tend to be alkaline but the water in Echinus is about as acidic as lemon juice and it is the largest frequently active acid geyser in the world.

The Bathtub is a thermal spring feature about 300 feet southwest of Black Growler steam vent in Norris Geyser Basin. It is a small geyser playing at intervals of a few minutes when active, otherwise boiling violently but throwing out no water. It received its name from the fact that it is a clear bubbling spring shaped like a bathtub.

The Norris Geyser Basin, the hottest geyser basin in the park, is located near the northwest edge of the Yellowstone Caldera near Norris Junction at the intersection of three major earthquake fault zones. This basin changes daily due to water fluctuations and seismic activity. New hot springs and geysers appear, others become dormant, and at times are closed off by park rangers if activity becomes too vigorous. The Norris Basin has it all: hot springs, geysers, fumeroles, and bubbling mudpots. This is a c. 1910 view of the Minute Man Geyser in eruption.

Constant Geyser in the past few years has been a relatively frequent performer, sometimes erupting every half hour or so in a quick, few-seconds burst spraying water 20 to 30 feet high. It is said that if you blink, you might miss it. Black Growler steam vent is on the hill slope to the right. It is a superheated steam vent, meaning the temperature of the steam is well above 212 degrees, the normal boiling point of water.

A close-up view of the Black Growler steam vent is shown in this 1954 postcard view. Notwithstanding its name, the Black Growler steam vent roars out of a porcelain-white orifice. This superheated steam vent has switched openings several times since it was first observed many years ago.

Valentine Geyser and Ledge Geyser are neighbors in the Norris Geyser Basin. Both are shown at play in this 1932 postcard view. Although both geysers reach 60 to 75 feet, they are independent of one another. Ledge is more active, usually playing three times a day, while Valentine's eruption interval varies from 18 hours to three days.

The milky color of the minerals deposited here inspired the naming of this area as Porcelain Basin. The mineral siliceous sinter is brought to the surface by hot water and forms a sinter sheet as the water flows across the ground and the mineral settles out. If the mineral deposit seals off a hot spring or geyser by plugging its vent, the hot, pressurized water may flow underground to a weaker area and blow through it.

Virginia Cascades on the Gibbon River courses down into a densely forested canyon. It is not a cataract but appears more as a slide, down which the water pours with great speed for a stretch of about 100 feet over the course of its 60-foot drop.

Gibbon Falls is located on the Gibbon River about midway between Norris Geyser Basin and Madison Junction. It is a long and ribbon-like cascade tumbling and dropping about 80 feet in a gradual descent. There is a parking area near the top of the falls, which offers a great viewpoint. The area is often crowded with sightseers.

The Gibbon Geyser Basin along the Gibbon River consists of four separate areas, each small but unique. Sylvan Springs Group contains many small acidic hot springs, including Evening Primrose Spring. Artist Paint Pots bubble and boil in colors of gray and pink. There is also a grouping of several small constant geysers. Monument Geyser Basin is unique in that tree trunk–like cones stand upright in a barren and desolate basin.

Beryl Spring, located in the Gibbon Geyser Basin, is a showy thermal feature, as it is one of the hottest springs in Yellowstone. It has a boiling, frothing hot pool or two; fissures from which smelly, sulfur gasses escape in pressured, jet-engine fashion and it exudes enough water vapor into the air to create small clouds that lift into the sky. It was named for the blue-green color of the gemstone beryl.

This 1910 RPPC image shows the soldier station at Nez Perce Creek, one of approximately 18 military sites that had been established by this time. Nez Perce Creek connects with the Firehole River just south of Madison Junction. This creek is named for Chief Joseph's tribe ("the pierced noses"), which passed this way in the summer of 1877 during its famous flight from the US Calvary before being captured in the Bearpaw Mountains of northern Montana.

The Fountain Hotel, built in 1891 as a stop for stagecoach visitors, was closed in 1916 when the advent of motorized transportation made it an unnecessary stopping point. After it was torn down in 1927, a salvage effort was made using some of the windows, doors, and lumber for the construction of a girls' dormitory at Old Faithful. The traditional Formation Dances were originated here at Norris, where ball gown and formal dress were required. It was here also that the practice of feeding kitchen garbage to the bears was begun. Bear viewing took place in the evenings after the refuse was hauled to the dumpsite. Fences were employed to keep people out of the feeding grounds; for, as explained by park employees, "Yes, bears are dangerous!" Fountain Geyser (below) erupts to a height of 50 feet, and eruptions last as long as an hour.

For those on the "grand tour," the Fountain Hotel was an important stopping place. The customary route traveled to the Upper Basin, and then travelers doubled back to this spot to stay the night. The next day, the tour group would be moved on to Lake Hotel. The hotel was built strategically facing the Fountain Geyser.

Fountain Paint Pots were called Mammoth Paint Pots by turn-of-the-century tourists, and it is one of the many mudpot areas in the park. In early summer, the mudpots are thin and watery from abundant rain and snow, which allows them to boil. Then by late summer, they thicken, creating unusual shapes and formations.

The postcard above shows the image of the only known photograph capturing an eruption of Excelsior Geyser. Frank J. Haynes and his family happened to be lunching nearby when they heard rumblings. Though a quarter mile away, Haynes quickly set up a camera and captured this image in 1888. Below, US Army troops are seen walking in the Midway Geyser Basin, near Excelsior Geyser. These troops may have been stationed at the Nez Perce Creek Camp, several miles to the north, or possibly at the Old Faithful Camp, several miles to the southeast.

White Dome Geyser (above) is conspicuous, as its 12-foot-high geyserite cone is one of the largest in the park. Its eruptions, attaining heights of about 30 feet, are unpredictable but generally occur with intervals ranging from 15 minutes to three hours. An image of the geyser is used today in the emblem of the Yellowstone Association. Shown below is a view of Middle Geyser Basin, taken from a c. 1885 stereograph published by Frank J. Haynes. This basin contains a small collection of mammoth-sized springs. Midway is part of the Lower Geyser Basin, but because of its isolated location between the main features of Lower and Upper geyser basins, it became known as Midway. Rudyard Kipling, who visited Yellowstone in 1889, is said to have immortalized this basin by referring to it as "Hell's Half Acre." Even today, it is occasionally remembered by that name.

This unidentified dog seemed to be enjoying his Yellowstone Park vacation. Fresh air and a great view were provided for this canine visitor riding in his cozy carrier attached to the side of an early touring car.

This 1936 RPPC image by Livingston photographer John Haberstroh shows a great close-up of a buffalo eating alfalfa on a snow-covered field in Yellowstone. Haberstroh was probably able to approach this buffalo fairly closely to take this picture, as these animals tend to be much more docile in the park's winter season.

Four

Old Faithful and the Upper Geyser Basin

This 1909 postcard is quite unusual for two reasons. The first is the subject matter. Close interaction between man and bear, now prohibited, was always potentially dangerous. The two people in the background are wisely keeping their distance. The second unusual thing about this card is that it is a true stereograph. The two images are just slightly offset and will merge into a single three-dimensional image when viewed through a stereoscope.

This 1921 postcard was published by Jack E. Haynes and is captioned "Old Faithful Camp, Yellowstone Park." Three tents are partially visible at the far left. This camp was in operation from 1898 into the 1920s, and it evolved into the Old Faithful Lodge, which opened in 1928.

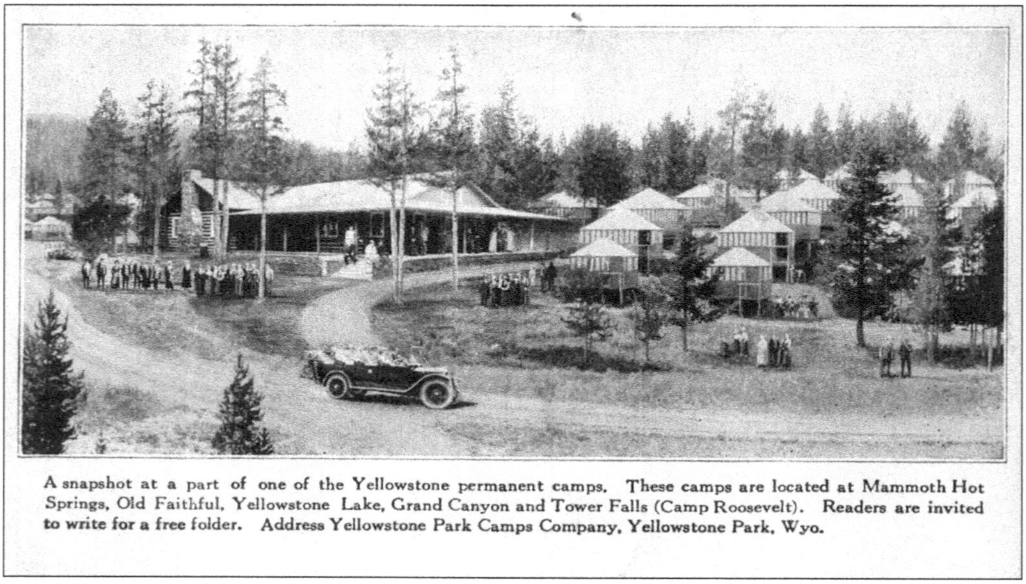

Taken at the Wylie Old Faithful Camp, this c. 1920 view was published by the Yellowstone Park Camps Company. Its advertising reads, "A snapshot at a part of one of the Yellowstone permanent camps. These camps are located at Mammoth Hot Springs, Old Faithful, Yellowstone Lake, Grand Canyon and Tower Falls (Camp Roosevelt). Readers are invited to write for a free folder. Address Yellowstone Park Camps Company, Yellowstone Park, Wyo."

Old Faithful Geyser owes it popularity to its fidelity, not to its height or beauty. In the early years, various geysers were soaped in an effort to produce eruptions. Even then, Old Faithful could not be shaken out of its near clock-like routine of erupting about every 65 minutes. A bit slower today, it still plays at fairly regular intervals. Experts say the interval to the next eruption can be calculated based on the total duration of the current eruption.

The Wylie Permanent Camping Company, whose main office was based outside the park, at Livingston, Montana, published this card about 1908. The caption reads, "Upper Geyser Basin Camp, Y. N. P. of Wylie P. Camping Co." A message penned on the back says, "Are having a fine trip. Our tent is the one with the cross. Have had good weather most of the way." This camp was set up near the Old Faithful Inn.

Dating from c. 1910, this RPPC captured the US Army camp set up in the Old Faithful area. The photographer, possibly one of the soldiers within this troop, waited for just the right moment to take this shot. Old Faithful can be seen erupting through the trees on the left side of this image.

Here, a 1910 RPPC shows a critical unit of any military operation: the mess tent. Several unidentified US Army soldiers, including one with an apron, pose for this picture, which is captioned "Hdqr. Kitchen." The park location of this scene is not certain, but it may be the Old Faithful military camp.

What could be more appropriate than America's national pastime in America's first national park? Captioned "Ball Game – Old Faithfull," this 1910 RPPC image shows soldiers and civilians partaking in a game of baseball. Again, the photographer has added an extra touch to this shot by capturing Old Faithful in action at the right.

Evening entertainment made for a fitting end to a fun-filled day in Yellowstone. The caption on the back includes the following: "Campfire Entertainment, Yellowstone Park. There were eleven hundred persons around this campfire when this picture was taken." Each of the major lodges—including Mammoth, Lake, Canyon and Old Faithful—featured varied and fun evening activities.

The c. 1910 image above shows two stagecoaches near the front entrance of the Old Faithful Inn. Constructed in 1903–1904, it was once the largest building of its kind in the world. Built entirely of logs, the lodge features interior decoration consisting of twisted tree limbs and gnarled trunks. The inn has repeatedly been remodeled and renovated, with an east wing added in 1913, the dining room enlarged in 1922, and then a west wing addition in 1927–1928. In celebration of the inn's centennial in 2004, a major multimillion-dollar renovation project was completed. Another c. 1910 view below shows the lobby and fireplace in the Old Faithful Inn. The stone fireplace is actually four fireplaces in one, sharing one great stone chimney. Each fireplace is large enough to hold four-foot sticks of wood, and guests are able to sit in front of a fire on whichever side they choose to enjoy. An iron clock designed by architect Robert C. Reamer hangs over the mantle on the fireplace chimney and has a pendulum that is 14 feet long.

Jack E. Haynes published this 1937 postcard showing the Art Deco–style interior, in keeping with the fashion of that era, exhibited in the Bear Pit cocktail lounge in the Old Faithful Inn. The lounge was decorated with wild animal scenes on wood wall panels, most of which included a touch of humor.

Highly popular today are the wintertime snowmobile and snowcoach tours, based mainly out of West Yellowstone. Some of these tours travel to the Grand Canyon and others to Old Faithful, allowing visitors to experience the winter beauty of the park as shown in this c. 1960 postcard.

Soldiers, likely stationed at the nearby Old Faithful military camp, pose for a picture near the edge of Riverside Geyser in this c. 1910 RPPC image. Note the stagecoach in the left background. Located along the Firehole River, Riverside is a crowd favorite that is widely photographed. Its eruption sprays as high as 75 feet, and it shoots water at an angle over the river, sometimes creating a rainbow effect. Riverside is one of the most predictable geysers in the park, erupting about four times a day.

Frank J. Haynes published this 1916 view captioned "Beehive Geyser, Yellowstone Park." This geyser is aptly named, as its four-foot-tall cone resembles a beehive. Beehive was one of seven geysers in the Upper Geyser Basin seen in the eruption phase and then named by the Washburn-Langford-Doane Expedition in 1870. Today, its eruptions last about five minutes and are 200 feet high. As of summer 2009, Beehive was having predictable eruptions every 11 to 14 hours.

In this 1952 view, cars are parked and ready for a "drive-in" viewing of Daisy Geyser at play. Another Upper Geyser Basin favorite, Daisy Geyser erupts every two to four hours for a period of three to five minutes and is one of the most predictable geysers in the park. Its fountain erupts at an angle and reaches heights of 75 feet. Daisy's eruption interval can be temporarily altered by an eruption at nearby Splendid Geyser.

A popular site in the Upper Geyser Basin, Oblong Geyser is so named because its crater is oblong in shape, measuring about 30 feet by 50 feet. Instead of spouting as most other geysers do, the entire pool of water is raised up in the air during an eruption, followed for several minutes by clouds of steam. This geyser then refills slowly, allowing an excellent view of the spherical masses of beautiful geyserite lining its interior.

In keeping with a National Park Service policy decision that no form of artificial recreational activities be allowed in the parks, it was decreed that the Hamilton pool and bathhouse (above) at Old Faithful be destroyed in 1949. The decision ordered that all traces be removed, with proper restoration then taking place. Hamilton fought the Washington decision, and the structure remained until the summer of 1951. "Natural" asphalt now covers the "artificial" pool.

People flocked to this awe-inspiring playground as stronger law enforcement began to bring stability and protection to the park's natural resources and wildlife. Whenever people travel, business opportunities beckon, and C.A. Hamilton purchased his first store, located at Old Faithful, in 1915. As he built more store concessions and fillings stations, Hamilton's genius at retail filled the need for general mercantile stores. It was here that treats and trinkets, the absolutes of the tourist trade, could be purchased.

Jack E. Haynes published this view in 1922. Text printed on the back includes the following: "The American Bison, commonly known as buffaloes, were driven to the mountain country during the great slaughtering of pioneer days and in the Yellowstone are increasing rapidly in numbers due, to their good care and protection." In August 2010, the National Park Service released a report that listed a population of approximately 3,900 buffalo.

Printed in 1914 by Frank J. Haynes, this card is captioned "No. 512 – Grand Geyser, Upper Basin – Yellowstone Park." This card is from a 50-card set called the 500 Series, as the cards are numbered from 501 to 550. Grand Geyser is the tallest and most spectacular of the predictable geysers. It erupts from a pool of water, making it a fountain-type geyser. Grand usually performs two or three times daily, reaching a height of 150 to 180 feet.

Giant Geyser was one of seven geysers in the Upper Geyser Basin that was seen in the eruption phase and then named by the Washburn-Langford-Doane Expedition in 1870. Its activity level varies considerably from year to year, and it sometimes goes long periods between eruptions. In recent times, there have been years with no eruptions and other years of up to 50 or more eruptions. When Giant does erupt, the activity can last over an hour and reach heights of 250 feet.

Scheuber Drug Company of Livingston, Montana, published this 1908 view of Sponge Geyser. Text printed on the back includes the following: "On Geyser Hill in Upper Basin, is the 'Sponge' so called from its close resemblance to an enormous sponge. Its steaming contents and porous walls attract the attention of all tourists. It is one of the smallest geysers with most eruptions varying between six to nine inches and wellings reaching two feet."

Morning Glory Pool is one of the most beautiful blue pools in the park, showing the colors and shape of a giant flower. Located about 1.5 miles from Old Faithful Geyser, this funnel-shaped pool measures roughly 23 feet across, and it is nearly 29 feet deep. The coloring is not from the water's mineral content but from its purity and the light color of the basin. Algae growing around the edges of the pool create the brown-tan framework.

Even the soldiers checked out geysers with close eyes as Castle Geyser underwent "inspection" in this 1910 RPPC. This geyser was named for its "resemblance to the ruins of an old castle." The large sinter cone is nearly 12 feet high. Before the 1959 earthquake, Castle was an irregular geyser, with periods of dormancy. Since then, it has become predictable, erupting every nine to 11 hours at up to 60 to 90 feet high for as long as one hour. (Courtesy of Hal Ottaway.)

Early park visitors often let their curiosity get the best of them, taking undue risks such as this man peeking into the chamber of Grotto Geyser. One of the most photographed geysers in the park because of its interesting shape, Grotto usually erupts every two to five hours and hits heights of 20 to 30 feet. Today, visitors are required to stay on boardwalks or other specified walkways as they view the thermal areas.

In 1908, the Scheuber Drug Company of Livingston, Montana, published this view of Biscuit Basin. Text printed on the back includes the following: "This weird spot is on the west bank of the Fire Hole River, over a mile below the entrance to the Upper Basin. Here the tourist finds the beautiful sapphire pool amidst a maze of biscuit-like knobs."

One of the more famous landmarks in the Upper Geyser Basin, Punchbowl Springs (also known as Devil's Punch Bowl), does not spout but keeps up an incessant boiling action. When a Wylie Camp was set up nearby in the early 1900s, this spring was used to supply hot water for the campers—to the detriment of the spring.

There are two places, in full view of the main highways, where it is common to see baby eagles, as in this c. 1910 view. One is located on the approach to Madison Junction. Here, parent birds are often seen going to and fro from their nest. Visitors are not allowed to encroach within certain posted areas. There is also a pinnacle in Gardiner Canyon called Eagles Nest Rock where the birds can be spotted.

This c. 1922 view was published by Jack E. Haynes and shows children and adults playing at Handkerchief Pool. It was a popular attraction at the time. Passersby would place a handkerchief into the pool, which was typically sucked down and then back up by the current, returning in "cleaned" condition. Unfortunately, visitors threw rocks, sticks and other objects into the pool, and it became clogged and no longer functional in 1928.

May through June is the time of year in the park that a visitor is most likely to see a bison cow feeding her calf. Visitors taking the walking tour of the Upper Geyser Basin and Old Faithful often encounter buffalo in small groupings. Observing buffalo (from a safe distance) is one of the highlights of a trip to Yellowstone.

Five

Yellowstone Lake and Its Sights

Lone Star Geyser has long intrigued people, inspiring the fellow in this c. 1885 stereograph to do some climbing (now illegal) on its 12-foot-high cone. This geyser is located in the Lone Star Geyser Basin, a backcountry region of pools and geysers close to the Firehole River. It erupts regularly and predictably about every three hours, blasting steam and water up to 50 feet in the air. The performances last up to 30 minutes, in several distinct phases of activity.

The Kepler Cascades, a few miles southeast of Old Faithful, fall 150 feet over multiple drops. Gustavus Doane, a member of the Washburn-Langford-Doane Expedition of 1870, wrote about the falls: "These pretty little falls, if located on an eastern stream, would be celebrated in history and song; here, amid objects so grand as to strain conception and stagger belief, they were passed without a halt." The cascades are shown here in a c. 1915 RPPC view.

The West Thumb Lunch Station was operated for stagecoach tourists traveling between West Thumb and Old Faithful. For those wishing to tarry, it did have a few overnight rooms available. Built in 1901, it operated as a lunch-stop up until 1917, when motorized transportation ended its usefulness. In 1912, three soldiers stopped by to drink and play cards. A fight ensued and, although a crisis was averted, the liquor stock was removed. The building was demolished in 1927.

The Fountain Paint Pots are located at West Thumb. The area resembles some vast boiling pot of paint with a continuous bubbling up of mud, producing sounds like a hoarsely whispered "plop, plop, plop." Hemispherical masses of cones, jets, and rings are colored gray, pink, and rose. In the spring, the mud is thin, and the pots boil. By fall, there is less moisture, and the mud is thicker, creating unusual formations.

Fishing Cone, also called Spring Cone, is located in Yellowstone Lake and rises and falls with the lake water level. A lava dome exists deep under the lake's northern end. As the dome swells and recedes the famous hot spring cone alternately is left high and dry or inundated, denoting the volcanic activity going on deep beneath the water. Visitors were once able to catch a fish in the lake and then cook it in the cone, while still on the line in just a few minutes.

The Natural Bridge is located south of Bridge Bay Campground. It was formed by waters of Bridge Creek naturally eroding the rhyolite outcrop. The top 51 feet above the creek can be reached by a short trail. To protect the feature, travel across the bridge is prohibited. This is a rare stereograph postcard published in 1909 by S.D. Butcher & Son.

Lake Hospital once supported a 10-bed acute care facility and served as an outpatient clinic in Yellowstone National Park. It used photophone teleradiology systems to send video pictures of injuries sustained by park visitors to specialists at other locations. This hospital has been replaced by an urgent-care facility. Clinics have been replacing hospitals in national parks as a way to save money while still providing emergency medical care.

The arrival of the automobile in 1916 created a great influx of visitors. The need arose for an intermediate style of lodging between the luxury of the Lake Hotel and the rustic accommodations of the tent camps. In 1926, the Lake Lodge, a Robert Reamer design and one of four lodges in the park, was completed. Yellowstone was no longer primarily accessible to only affluent dudes or hearty sagebrushers. Democracy had come to the park.

One of the most distant camps from its base at Fort Yellowstone in Mammoth, the Lake Army camp is shown here in a c. 1910 RPPC image. This site, near Yellowstone Lake, was one of 18 military camps set up in the park by the US Army during its 32-year tenure in Yellowstone. Hardy soldiers lived under these primitive conditions year-round in some of these tent camps.

Whether one was of military or civilian status, a busy day in Yellowstone Park was always an appetite-builder. These c. 1910 views provide a contrasting look at dining preparations. The card above shows a military "kitchen" with a cook in apron posing with fellow troops at the tent entrance. Probably at the Lake Army Camp, this cook is about to prepare a string of freshly caught fish from Yellowstone Lake. The image below shows the interior of a Wylie Dining Tent, with places set for soon-to-arrive tourists. The Wylie Tent Camping Company had permanent tent camps all over the park, including one at Lake. These colorful tents could be considered fancy for a tent experience, having wooden floors and some solid furniture with nice bedding. At mealtime, people would dress to the hilt, attired in their Sunday-best clothes to go down and eat.

Here are two postcards with views depicting the experience of "doing the grand tour" by the lodge system as opposed to going first-class to the grand Lake Hotel. The view above shows the dining room area in the lodge. In 1924, the kitchen was enlarged and two wings were added in 1926 that included the cafeteria and recreation hall, which was used to host dances and shows, as well. The view below shows the dining room in the Lake Hotel. Opened in 1893 and renovated by Robert Reamer beginning in 1903, this double-colonnaded dining room off the hotel lobby today offers one of the most elegant dining experiences in the park. In addition to the food, it offers an expansive view of the lake stretching south. This vast dining room does not even feel crowded when full, allowing for a relaxed atmosphere.

YELLOWSTONE LAKE, YELLOWSTONE NATIONAL PARK.

5117. COPYRIGHT, 1900, BY DETROIT PHOTOGRAPHIC CO.

Yellowstone Lake, covering some 136 square miles, is up to 390 feet deep and is the largest freshwater lake above 7,000 feet in North America. In recent years, much news has been generated by the discovery of volcanic activity taking place beneath the apparently calm waters. Fish have died from sulfuric gas emissions and rising water temperatures, and it was confirmed in 1983 that the north end of the lake has undergone uplift and that the south end of the lake has tilted downward, turning what was once a peninsula into an island. Below the water lies what is thought to be one of the largest volcanic calderas in the world, generating much media attention to this "super volcano." According to a 1909 travel guide, the Hofer Boat Company maintained a complete outfit of small launches, rowboats, and such at the lake.

No. 168 BOAT LANDING NEAR LAKE HOTEL – YELLOWSTONE PARK. HAYNES-PHOTO. Printed in Germany.

The steamboat *E.C. Waters*, the largest ever to ply the lake, was built on site by E.C. Waters. In 1896, he brought four bison along with a few elk and bighorn sheep to Dot Island, where he intended to use them to attract tourists. Failing to obtain government approval to carry his desired 500 passengers per trip, he left the new ship to rot on the shore of Stevenson Island. In 1926, the boiler was removed and then used to heat the Lake Hotel for 46 years.

The lake was a source of tall tales related by tour guides. When unsuspecting fishermen inquired about the fish population, they were obligingly informed that only a few had survived a cloudburst that had drowned almost all of them. Therefore, the remaining fish grew to unusual size because they had so much room. Another story went, "A feller caught one so big, it took three days for the water to fill up the hole it came out of." Oblivious to tall tales, these pelicans enjoy the lake.

The Lake Hotel was once a large three-story building, a simple box-like structure with projecting dormers at each end. Its was originally built to serve stagecoach guests brought to the park by the Northern Pacific Railway, with the hotel's construction being supervised for the railroad by R.R. Cummins. During its first series of remodeling in 1903–1905, the lodging was redesigned and substantially expanded by Robert Reamer. At this time, an eastward extension was added with a third matching portico. The building was transformed from a plain, box-shaped structure into a luxury, colonial-style building of beauty. Today, it retains the classic yellow-and-white exterior color scheme introduced at that time. Below is a c. 1905 image showing the lobby area.

As the hotel was once a much simpler building in appearance, there are those that feel that the 1903–1905 remodeling that brought the stately porticoes with Ionic columns and neoclassical touches to the building made the Lake Hotel seem out of place in the woodsy, natural environment provided by Yellowstone Park. The controversy over the question of appropriate architectural design and function has continued to this day. Presently, it is still an elegant colonial-style structure as well as the oldest standing hotel in the park. Preliminary archeological studies indicate that indigenous people inhabited the Lake area 9,600 years ago. Numerous projectile points have been found in addition to a hearth (cooking) structure, middens, and a bison-harvest site. The image below shows the Lake Hotel Lounge in the 1930s.

The Lake Camp or Lake Lodge, as it was also referred to, was another of the structures designed by Robert Reamer. A rustic lodge, it was built in 1919–1920 on the site of the former Wylie Camping Company. Located near the Yellowstone Lake Outlet, the structure was situated in a wooded location. The concept of the complex was similar to that of the other camp lodges located throughout the park. At first, guests slept in "permanent" tents that featured wood floors and were comfortably set up with beds and simple furniture. If one looks to the right in the postcard image above, the tents that were moved to Lake during this time are visible. Eventually, in the 1930s, these tents were replaced by rustic wood cabins. Both accommodations were conveniently placed in proximity to the main building, where basic services were offered. The lobby at Lake Lodge later featured log tables for dining and a large stone fireplace. Dancing and shows were presented in the nearby recreation hall to entertain the guests.

The construction of the core of the Lake Hotel was begun in 1889 on the shores of Yellowstone Lake, where the hotel commanded a beautiful view of lake. Its early-1900s transformation by architect Reamer was but the first of its renovations. In 1922–1923, a further three-story extension to the east was added, this with a flat roof. In 1928, a two-story west wing was added, expanding the dining room and adding a solarium to the front. All are visible in this 1950s postcard.

Lakeshore Geyser is located on the shore of Yellowstone Lake but is in fact inundated by cold lake water most of the time, rendering the geyser dormant. It can only erupt on those occasions when the lake is low and the geyser is hot. This is a fairly rare occurrence, and the geyser has long periods of dormancy. When in eruption, the water column reaches 20 to 30 feet high, which over a period of 10 minutes gradually decreases in force.

The Lake Museum is located near the Fishing Bridge Camp Ground on the edge of Yellowstone Lake. The museum has exhibits of lake wildlife within. Outside, nearby, there is an amphitheater where lectures are given.

Fishing Bridge gains its name from a 1902 bridge that once served as Yellowstone's most popular angling location. During the park's early history, throngs of fishermen would crowd this small fishing hole, which was popular for cutthroat trout. The area was closed to fishing in 1973 because the bridge crossed the Yellowstone River above a cutthroat trout spawning ground.

The area surrounding Fishing Bridge is a jumble of historic and natural wonders. There are many trails and, due to bear activity in the area, the campground there is limited to hard-sided vehicles only. Today at Bridge Bay Marina, boat rides around Stevenson Island are available, and it is possible to rent fishing gear and small powerboats. Lake trout were one of the first nonnative species introduced into Yellowstone, beginning in 1889. Having made their way into Yellowstone Lake, they are now considered an invasive species, and efforts to eradicate them have literally netted nearly a half a million fish in the past few years. Old fish stories at Lake Yellowstone may be taken at their face value: the biggest one never got away, because they, the fish, were all about the same size, and it was useless to lie about the number caught because the truth was enough, and more than 25 meant jail.

This 1923 postcard view published for the Northern Pacific Railway, is captioned "Setting the Table for Bears at Lake Camp, Yellowstone Park." This brave young lady is shown preparing a table setting for young bears, who will hopefully maintain good table manners until food is served and the hostess has scampered up the hill to a safe vantage point.

Bears always loved free, easy meals, which for a time were supplied by park employees. Garbage from the hotel and lodge kitchens was hauled by wagons out to Greek theater–style dumpsites near Old Faithful and Canyon Lodges during the early 1900s. The bears pawed through the leftovers as though being served gourmet meals, and tourists were thrilled by their antics. Armed US Army troops (shown here) and, later, park rangers patrolled the out-of-bounds areas.

Once a mound, Mud Volcano tore itself apart and became the formation that is seen today. Named in 1871 by the Hayden Expedition, it was a very active mud spring with bellowing and exploding mud. It quieted down until 1979, when a series of minor earthquakes increased its heat and water activity. For a short while, it went through a period of bursting and spilling mud across the boardwalks.

Dragon's Mouth is a turbulent hot spring, 16 feet deep, with a cavernous mouth. Water sloshes rhythmically in and out of the cavern giving the impression of a large overflow although the actual discharge is quite small. Most of the activity and energy is located within. As hot water rises to the surface, the gases expand, creating a pressure explosion in the cavern. The result is the sloshing, belching, and steaming witnessed by visitors.

The natural meandering of Trout Creek in the Hayden Valley forms the ancient pattern of the Chinese monad. The yin and yang, sometimes identified as the diagram of the "Great Extreme," is an expression of the duality of nature. This symbol was adopted by the Northern Pacific Railway as its trademark. The fishes of Yellowstone are an artificial assemblage of native and introduced species. The aquatic ecosystem has been forever altered by the introduction of nonnative species. Of the approximately 20 known species in park waters, 12 are natives. Not wanting to be left behind in the great hatchery revolution of the first half of the 20th century, park managers quickly added various strains of rainbows to their hatchery and stocking programs. They planted fish where there never were trout and in rivers where there were pristine populations of very rare native fish, changing forever the fish ecology of Yellowstone.

These images reflect a once common view of bears "working their roadside stand." Until 1965, "beggar" or "hold-up" bears frequented park roads, staking out panhandling spots. There, they waited for motoring tourists, who could not resist stopping. Throwing all caution aside and forgetting that these cute creatures were wild animals, people foolishly stepped out of their cars to offer tidbits and snap pictures. Such risks at times led to encounters that were much too close and personal with the oversized teddy. This practice led to such concern for the safety of Yellowstone tourists that many of the black bears had to be removed to backcountry areas of the park in order to protect tourists from their own folly.

The Hayden Valley is located six miles north of the Fishing Bridge Junction. Its large, open meadows are the remains of ancient lakebeds. The valley supports one of America's finest wildlife habitats and is covered with a variety of lush vegetation. Wildlife sightings here are frequent, and visitors are reminded to follow all safety tips as grizzly bears, bison, and elk all roam freely across the valley floor.

Within three years after the first automobile entered Yellowstone Park, the Mammoth Hot Springs Hotel sported a fleet of touring cars for availability. One such tour group, shown in this postcard image, crosses the original Chittenden Bridge spanning the Yellowstone River upstream from the Upper Falls. The introduction of automobiles into the park brought about the need for postcard publishers to produce new images for their card lines.

Six

From Canyon to the Valleys and Tower Falls

The US Army first arrived in Yellowstone Park in 1886 to deal with such issues as poaching and vandalism. Using their first tent camp at Mammoth as a base, soldiers established six other camps at strategic points within the park by the end of 1886. These camps included Soda Butte, Norris, Riverside, Fountain Flats, Old Faithful, and Grand Canyon, shown in this c. 1910 RPPC image, with 10 more being established by 1918.

During its 32-year presence in Yellowstone Park, the military had an overall very positive effect on the environment. When the first troops arrived, officials did not anticipate a lengthy stay. A long-term military presence became the policy, however, as protection and supervision of the park's large physical area by the Army was seen to be the best approach. In 1910, at the height of the Army's residence in Yellowstone, there were 324 soldiers here, along with families and civilian employees. These troops staffed not only Fort Yellowstone, but were stationed throughout the park in small details at various outposts. On this page are two c. 1910 RPPCs showing the Army in the Yellowstone. The card above is captioned "Camp Fire," and the image below is captioned "Cavalry Camp." In 1916, the National Park Service was established, and the Cavalry ceded control of Yellowstone to a civilian authority.

Bears have long caused concern for the safety of tourists in the park. A report written in 1905 by Major Pitcher states, "The bear are about the only animals that the summer tourists cannot fail to see. It is difficult to make some of the tourists realize that the bear in the Park are wild and that it is a dangerous matter to trifle with them." Up until the 1960s, bears freely wandered into cabin and house kitchens as they pleased. Careful storage of food in the campgrounds often proved a wasted effort. The card above, set in comic-style artwork, nonetheless imparts a serious message about the potential danger of bears to people inside or outside the park. The caption on the card below reads, "Cinnamon Bear in garbage can at Canyon Camp, July, 1918." (Below, courtesy of Francis Historical Collection.)

The Shaw & Powell Camping Company was run by Livingston businessman J.D. Powell and various members of the Shaw family. The outfit supplied camping and transportation facilities for tourists before the arrival of automobiles and buses into the park in 1916. This c. 1915 view shows the company's Canyon Camp building.

Shaw & Powell operated mobile camps on the basis of one-year leases from the Department of the Interior from 1898 until 1913. At that time, Shaw & Powell was granted a 10-year lease for seven permanent camps. This view shows the Canyon Camp Dining Room.

Canyon Lodge, also know as Canyon Camp, was built in the mid-1920s on the site of the old Shaw & Powell permanent tent camp located on the Artist's Point spur road. Included at this site was the large L-shaped main building constructed of logs and shingles. According to a 1941 description of the area, the Canyon Lodge complex offered a store, meals, cocktail lounge, beauty parlor, and barbershop. Each evening, park employees called "savages" presented programs in the spacious lobby, and dancing followed. Its rustic style of architecture was admirably adapted to the forest in which the lodge was situated. Remnants of this complex can still be found in the meadows. In 1915, the first automobiles were allowed into the park, and it became obvious that a new era had arrived. New lodging was begun to cater to and accommodate automobiles, while accommodations that catered to coach tours were removed.

The second Grand Canyon Hotel was in operation until 1910. It had been constructed in 1889 and was incorporated into and replaced by its grand successor, the new Canyon Hotel. This barn-like building contained 250 guest rooms and featured steam heat.

At first, the transportation of tourists through the park was an adjunct of the hotel business. In 1891, the Interior Department granted this privilege to a new company called the Yellowstone Park Transportation Company. "YPT Co" markings are visible on the front of a horse-drawn sled carrying a driver and one passenger shown in this c. 1912 RPPC view.

The New Grand Canyon hotel sat on a prominence 1,000 feet above the Lower Falls and was said to rival any resort hotel in the world. Measuring a mile around at its base, the hotel was an incredibly large building for its time. It contained all the conveniences of modern civilization and was considered an ideal place to spend a vacation. The Prairie Style hotel was designed by Robert Reamer. Guests descended from the reception desk down a shallow set of stairs and past a musician stand into the lounge where orchestras played nightly in the expansive lounge area. Built in 1911, the lodging became a casualty of the 1959 Hebgen earthquake when it was discovered that the foundations had been damaged to such an extent that repairing building was not economical. It was ordered razed, but before its dismantling could be completed, it mysteriously caught fire in 1960 and burned to the ground.

On the evening of August 17, 1959, a 7.5-magnitude earthquake centered at Hebgen Lake struck, and in split seconds a mountain was sheared off, as if some giant hand hurled an estimated 90 million tons of earth and boulders across the canyon, burying everything before it and creating a new lake. The quake was felt all over the Yellowstone area, and damage of varying degrees was widespread. Rocks roared down into the canyon at speeds of 174 miles per hour, permanently entombing an unknown number of campers beneath the landslide; their bodies were never recovered. Below, just a few miles below Hebgen Dam, Montana State Highway 1 submerges into the backwaters of Quake Lake, which was formed when the earthquake completely dammed the Madison River.

The view above shows the Main Canyon Village Lodge and administration buildings. These structures and 500 guest cottages represented an investment of more than $5 million. Begun in 1956, the village was in operation for the 1957 season. Proponents of its construction were of the belief that motorists would prefer to drive up to their cottages rather than park in a remote lot and carry their belongings up to their hotel rooms. To their embarrassment, tourists still seemed to prefer the old Canyon Hotel, resulting in the Canyon Hotel being closed down at the end of the 1958 season, forcing guests to stay in the new Canyon Village Lodge cabins. The image below shows an interior view of the new Canyon Village lounge, a modernistic room where soft background music was played.

The c. 1920 RPPC above shows an overlook once standing at the brink of the 109-foot-high Upper Falls of the Yellowstone River. Here, the river crashes through the Grand Canyon of the Yellowstone a short distance upstream from the Lower Falls. Curious tourists asking the early guides if the same amount of water flowed over both the Upper and the Lower Falls were sometimes given a tongue-in-cheek reply that more went over the Lower Falls. The reason given was that as the water flowed over the Upper Falls, it made one drop. Then a second drop was made as it thundered over the Lower Falls, so there was one drop more in the river when it went over the Lower Falls. A c. 1909 RPPC view of the Upper Falls is shown below, in a very unusual stereograph postcard format.

As the Yellowstone River flows north from Yellowstone Lake, it leaves the Hayden Valley and plunges first over Upper Yellowstone Falls and then, a quarter mile downstream, over Lower Yellowstone Falls, at which point it enters the Grand Canyon of the Yellowstone. In places, the canyon walls drop up to 1,000 feet to the river below. The Lower Falls is 308 feet high, or almost twice as high as Niagara Falls, and is the tallest falls in the park. The Lower Falls of the Yellowstone has a larger volume of water passing over it than any other waterfall in the Rocky Mountain area.

This was a common scene in the park prior to 1915: tourists sightseeing from a Concord stagecoach while being enlightened by a coach driver schooled in the art of tall tales. The drivers each commanded their own teams of horses and were very colorful. Here, the tour group is admiring the Upper Falls from an overlook of the Grand Canyon of the Yellowstone. Automobiles were allowed in the park in 1915, which resulted in the discontinuance of stagecoach travel.

In this picture from Artist Point, the Lower Falls of the Yellowstone, 308 feet in height, are a mile distant from the camera. Practically all park visitors make this side trip to Artist Point. This is often said to be the view Thomas Moran painted in his famous Grand Canyon of the Yellowstone.

36622 LOOKOUT ON WASHBURN MOUNTAIN, 10,317 FT. COPYRIGHT BY HAYNES INC., YELLOWSTONE PARK, WYO.

This c. 1937 view shows the stone lookout tower on the summit of Mount Washburn. The elevation of 10,317 feet given in the caption has been revised downward nearly 100 feet with modern measuring technology. Still, the road over Mount Washburn provides the highest elevation reached by automobile in the park. The highest point in Yellowstone is atop Eagle Peak, at 11,358 feet.

WASHBURN HOT SPRINGS, YELLOWSTONE NATIONAL PARK.

After passing over the summit of Dunraven Pass on the Grand Loop Road between Tower and Canyon, drivers approach an overlook at the Caldera Hot Springs Road. From there, the steam rising from the Washburn Hot Springs is visible in the nearby forests to the east. These extremely hot springs boil out of the caldera's fracture lines and are not accessible by foot, because the ground is too toxic and unstable.

The historic Roosevelt Lodge was named after Pres. Theodore Roosevelt. It was completed 17 years after his month-long camping visit near here in 1903. Roosevelt never actually visited the lodge. Overlooking the Lamar River and the Yellowstone River valleys, it is surrounded by the tranquil peace and quiet of the forest. The lodge building itself includes a dining room, lobby, registration area, and a long, wide porch lined with rocking chairs. It is a prime example of Old West style. There are approximately 80 log cabins for visitors located here. These accommodations are simple, with no frills, and are divided into the Frontier cabins and the Roughrider cabins. Frontier cabins are better equipped and include bathrooms. It is not known how many cabins were originally constructed at Roosevelt, but many cabins were moved there from other locations in the park.

With its wood and stone architecture highlighted by two stone fireplaces that create a cozy, quiet space, the Camp Roosevelt Lounge has a rugged but charming atmosphere compared to other area accommodations. It is much the same today as when built, with Old Hickory rocking chairs on the porch, an open dining area, and the inviting stone fireplaces. The fireplaces were eventually converted to gas logs.

The Roosevelt Lodge also provides exciting stagecoach rides along a two-mile route over scenic trails for up-close views of the landscapes and animals. These coaches are replicas of the original tallyho stages used until 1917 to transport visitors taking the Grand Tour of Yellowstone Park to and from the railroad depot in Gardiner to Mammoth Hot Springs.

The Tower Falls Store and Picture Shop, as shown in this c. 1923 view, served as one of several picture shops used by Jack E. Haynes within the park. Taking over the family business after his father, Frank J. Haynes, retired in 1916, Jack E. Haynes carried on the business of selling postcards, photographs, guides, and other park souvenirs for another 40 years, until his death in 1962.

This 1947 image shows a remnant of a once great primeval forest that stood at Specimen Ridge, on a spur road one-half mile south of the Tower Fall-Mammoth Highway. It stood protected from souvenir collectors by an iron fence. Modern studies have shown there to be 21 successive generations of trees. The age of this petrification is approximately 40 million years. Although the park has one of the world's largest petrified forests, this tree is a siliceous replica-fossil of an ancient redwood.

These ancient stumps on Specimen Ridge are of trees that lived millions of years ago. They were buried in volcanic ash and reappeared as the softer material surrounding them eroded away. There is an old Jim Bridger story about petrified agate wood pieces being gathered from a hidden, mysterious, totally petrified forest where petrified birds perched on petrified trees and petrified rabbits bounded among petrified bushes. Such was the fantasy forest he first reported in 1830.

This c. 1905 postcard was published by award-winning photographer W.S. Berry of Gardiner, Montana, and shows several Rocky Mountain bighorn sheep on a snow-covered hillside. Bighorn sheep have great balance and are comfortable on steep terrain and rocky ledges. They are found in the Mammoth Hot Springs–Gardiner area, Lamar Valley, and sometimes in the Tower Falls area as well as on Mount Washburn.

The entire region of the Needles, near Tower Falls, contains remarkable, almost man-made looking layers of basalt columns, pillars, and spires. So regular and uniform are the columns that they resemble posts in a picket stockade or bullets in a cartridge belt. Here, the east wall of the Grand Canyon, facing the overlook, is a cross-section of layers of glacial drift resting on lake deposits and columnar basalt. The columns were caused by cooling, shrinking, and cracking of several basaltic flows.

In this 1906 postcard image, Tower Creek falls 132 feet over a sheer cliff into a chasm where it eventually joins the Yellowstone River. The high breccia towers, from which the creek and falls take their names, rise from the head of the fall. Although one of the park's most spectacular falls, it requires a bit of a hike to reach, and, unfortunately, is one of the least visited of Yellowstone's major attractions.

The entire Tower Falls region is an area of stone columns, spires, and pillars that in places resemble broken columns from an Egyptian temple or the spires of some medieval castle, with stone palisades and ramparts topped by parapets. In 1975, an earthquake with an epicenter near Norris Geyser Basin shook the Yellowstone region. It brought down delicate spires in the Grand Canyon, and along this rim, large rockfalls tumbled down the canyon, nearly striking passing hikers.

Bighorn Sheep are named for the large, curved horns borne by the rams. Ewes also have horns, but they are shorter, with less curvature. Around 1800, bighorn sheep were widespread, with their North American population at around two million. Hunting and disease combined to reduce their population to just a few thousand by 1900. Bighorns have made a comeback with the help of good wildlife management programs and park protections. Still, there are fewer than 500 bighorn sheep in the park today.

Camp Roosevelt, located on or very near the site of today's Roosevelt Lodge, included wood-floored tents with basic furniture and a single large tent for dining. Wylie Camps were particularly popular among tent-campers and sometimes even lodge guests because of their nightly campfire entertainment. Every evening, staffers, often college students on summer break, would put on skits and stage sing-alongs around a campfire. Although simple and amateurish, the staff entertainment prompted camaraderie and interaction among the guests. Camp Roosevelt and other Wylie Camps had other charms. Early each morning, a staffer would quietly enter each tent and build a fire in the woodstove so guests awoke to a warm tent. Being on staff at a camp meant being a jack-of-all-trades, and every tent camp had one staff person whose job it was to man the dining tent armed with bats and shovels to fight off the bears when they visited in search of an easy dinner.

Private automobiles were first allowed into the park in August 1915. The following year, free camps with tap water and pit toilets were built in some areas. By 1919, over half of the tourists entering Yellowstone by automobile came prepared to camp. This prompted the construction of many additional public auto camps. Soon to follow, in the 1920s, were facilities to cater to the campers, such as stores and food supply establishments. Those who preferred to avoid the larger public camps were encouraged to look for designated smaller roadside campsites. The c. 1920 RPPC image above is captioned "Camp near Tower Falls, Y. N. Park." Below is a c. 1925 image published by Jack E. Haynes and captioned "A Yellowstone Public Automobile Camp, Yellowstone Park." (Above, courtesy of Francis Historical Collection.)

John C. Haberstroh of Livingston, Montana, was one of the finest Yellowstone Park postcard photographers. In this c. 1936 RPPC image, Haberstroh captured a "coyote calling" skyward in snowy terrain. Known for his sharp, high-contrast photographs, Haberstroh excelled in capturing Yellowstone National Park wildlife on his postcard images for a period of over 20 years.

A favorite theme of postcard senders in early days were cards showing human interaction with bears in Yellowstone. This c. 1930 RPPC image is an especially appealing view in which the elements of risk-taking abound. Hopefully, this man kept his balance and dropped the tidbit safely into the bear's mouth, and the contented bear ambled off with a happy ending. Although incidents of injury and death were seldom, they did occur, and restrictions on interactions with wildlife were enacted in the 1960s. (Courtesy of Francis Historical Collection.)

Seven

Gateways to Wonderland

The Flagg Ranch, featured in this 1958 postcard, is the last stop for motorists before they enter the southern entrance to Yellowstone Park. This Wyoming lodge is positioned two miles south of Yellowstone National Park and five miles north of Grand Teton National Park. Scenes of both parks are shown in the lower half of the card.

Livingston, Montana, 60 miles north of Yellowstone Park, was a mainline hub for the Northern Pacific Railway from the time of its creation in 1882. The following year, a branch line was built that ran south through Paradise Valley to Cinnabar, three miles from the park. In 1902, the line was extended to Gardiner. This 1940 RPPC shows the second Livingston depot. The station billed itself as the "Original Gateway to Yellowstone Park."

The Paradise Valley fills much of the corridor between Livingston and Gardiner. Famous for fishing and natural hot springs, the valley's attractions include Chico Hot Springs, La Duke Hot Springs, and Hunter's Hot Springs. This 1908 RPPC view shows a group of guests, young and old, posed for a picture on the porch of the new Chico Hot Springs Hotel. Among the guests who visited the hotel were Teddy Roosevelt and artist Charlie Russell.

Corwin Springs, 15 miles north of Gardiner, was another important tourist stop in the Paradise Valley in the early days. The Corwin train stop served as the stop-off for guests going to Dick Randall's OTO Ranch, one of Montana's oldest and most famous dude ranches. An interior view of the ranch house is shown here, postmarked from Duderanch, Montana, in 1933.

This RPPC view shows Gardiner's Front Street in the early 1950s. The arch is visible at the far left. Gardiner was founded in 1880 and is the original and the only year-round entrance for park visitation. The Yellowstone National Park Heritage and Research Center, which opened in 2005, is located in Gardiner, and houses National Park Service archives, Yellowstone museum collections, and reference libraries.

This 1930 poster art image, captioned "Gardiner Gateway, Yellowstone Park," was published by the Northern Pacific Railway. The card was part of a series of at least a dozen postcards issued by the railroad highlighting interesting locations and destinations it served throughout the Northwest. Many of these images also appeared on large posters or calendars. Railroad service to Gardiner was discontinued in 1948.

In 1903, the same year that the Northern Pacific depot opened at Gardiner, the Roosevelt Arch was constructed to serve as the northern entrance to the park. President Roosevelt was visiting Yellowstone at the time construction was beginning, and he was asked to place the cornerstone for the arch. In ceremony he did so, and the arch was given his name. This 1910 image shows a four-horse stagecoach at the entrance.

Here, a train is arriving at the Oregon Short Line depot at West Yellowstone, Montana. The Oregon Short Line, which began operations here in 1908, and the Union Pacific Railroad, which opened in 1909, brought thousands of Yellowstone visitors to West Yellowstone during the early decades of the 20th century. West Yellowstone had been made an official entrance to Yellowstone Park in 1907. By 1960, all railroad passenger train service to West Yellowstone ended.

Automobiles were first allowed into Yellowstone in 1915. The following year, the Yellowstone Park Transportation Company was awarded exclusive rights to operate public transportation in the park by the National Park Service. This 1925 RPPC image shows a serious-looking group aboard an open-air bus, hopefully ready to crack smiles and express delight as they experience the sights of the park's wonderland. As noted in the caption, these buses picked up their passengers at the Union Pacific station in West Yellowstone.

This West Yellowstone scene shows the Smith & Chandler store, founded in 1925. The building pictured here burned to the ground in the early 1970s but was rebuilt and continues to operate today as a popular gift shop.

Three unidentified men, dressed in the outdoor styles of the day, pose beside an early automobile. This RPPC image was taken in West Yellowstone about 1925, across the street from Eagle's Store and close to the park entrance. Signs for the Hotel Madison and the Hotel Teepee are visible in the right background.

Here are two views of West Yellowstone that show part of this gateway town as it looked during the 1930s and 1940s. Two of the town's prominent hotels, Hotel Tepee and Hotel Madison, are shown. Farther down the street are several cafés, a curio shop, and a Texaco gas station. The rightmost building is the Eagle's Store, shown in a close-up view below. Still one of the most prominent stores in West Yellowstone today, Eagle's featured a soda fountain, general merchandise, and a gas station out front. The same is true today, and the store is a true town landmark. Previously, the town's post office was also located there. As in the past, West Yellowstone's economy still relies heavily on tourism, as over a million people from around the world annually pass through what is now the most popular gateway for park visitors.

Spectators and hotel guests standing outside the Stage Coach Inn in West Yellowstone were treated to a "cutter race," captured in this 1968 image. During the winter months, according to the caption on the back, three or four cutter races were scheduled in West Yellowstone. Cutter races featured a pair of teams running two abreast. Each team consists of two horses, a driver, and a "chariot," and they usually raced for a quarter of a mile.

This 1945 RPPC image shows the West Gate to Yellowstone National Park. This entrance is now the busiest of the five entrances to the park. Also called the West Entrance, it is usually open from mid-April until the first of November for motorists. For winter activities, which include snowshoes, ski, snowmobile, or snowcoach access, this entrance is open from mid-December until mid-March.

This 1920 RPPC image shows the spiral bridge on the Cody Road to Yellowstone. This stretch of road was just a short distance inside the eastern entrance to the park on Sylvan Pass. At this point on the road grade, limited room made this loop an engineering necessity at the time. The weight requirements for carrying motor vehicles had made it necessary to build a concrete bridge (seen here) to replace the earlier wooden span. (Courtesy of Francis Historical Collection.)

This c. 1928 view of the "Eastern Entrance Gateway of Yellowstone National Park" was published by Jack E. Haynes. This gateway on the Cody Road was situated in the valley of Middle Creek, 27 miles from Yellowstone Lake and about 55 miles from Cody, Wyoming.

Tex Holms was one of Cody's most famous early guides. Holms billed himself as a "Pioneer Yellowstone Guide" and often took visitors into Yellowstone Park over the Cody Road. This 1909 image is captioned "In Camp with Tex Holms at Turbid Lake, Cody, Wyo." This scene is actually within the park. Turbid Lake is located near the northeast corner of Lake Yellowstone.

The high elevations in and around Yellowstone National Park result in heavy snowfall accumulations from November though April. This 1925 RPPC image, by photographer F. J. Hiscock of Cody, shows four tourists stopping to survey the deep snow from atop a snowbank. Three cars are dwarfed by this "Snow Cut" on Sylvan Pass, which is just inside the eastern entrance to the park on the Cody Road.

The scenic northeastern entrance to Yellowstone Park opened in 1937 with the completion of the Beartooth Highway. This road begins at Red Lodge, Montana, climbs to nearly 11,000 feet, and then drops into the towns of Cooke City and Silver Gate, near the park entrance. This 1915 RPPC shows part of Red Lodge's main street after a May snowstorm. With its lengthy snow season, this town of 2,500 people is a popular winter ski destination.

Construction of the Beartooth Highway between Red Lodge and Cooke City was completed in 1937 after about five years of work. Climbing out of Red Lodge on the way to Yellowstone, motorists are treated to one of the most picturesque mountain drives in America. A series of switchbacks climb 5,000 feet over a stretch of 15 miles out of Rock Creek Gorge. This is a c. 1934 RPPC view of construction work along one of the switchbacks.

Cooke City is on the other end of the Beartooth Highway, 65 miles from Red Lodge and only about 5 miles from the northeastern park entrance. This 1948 RPPC image shows a view of this charming little town, which boasts slightly over 100 residents.

This 1945 RPPC view shows the Silver Gate entrance to Yellowstone, busy with cars going in both directions. About a mile from this gate is the small town of Silver Gate, Montana. Since 1932, Silver Gate has served as a gateway to Yellowstone. Heading into the park from this entrance leads the motorist into the Lamar Valley, one of the best wildlife venues in Yellowstone.

Bibliography

Barber, John F. *Old Yellowstone Views*. Missoula, MT: Mountain Press Publishing Company, 1987.

Dougherty, Michael, Heidi Pfeil Dougherty, Kristin E. Hill, Lauri Olsen, and Ultimate Press Staff. *The Ultimate Yellowstone Atlas and Travel Encyclopedia*. Bozeman, MT: Ultimate Press, 2006.

Francis, Michael H., Kathleen M. Burke, and J. Michael Bodell. *Yellowstone Postcard Checklist*. Self-published, 2006.

Karle, Marsha, Lee H. Whittlesey, and the Yellowstone Staff. *A Yellowstone Album*. Lanham, MD: Roberts Rinehart Publishers, 1997.

Meyer, Judith L. *The Spirit of Yellowstone*. Lanham, MD: Roberts Rinehart Publishers, 2003.

Milstein, Michael. *Yellowstone: 125 Years of America's Best Idea*. Billings, MT: The Billings Gazette, 1996.

Nolan, Edward W. *Northern Pacific Views: The Railroad Photography of F. Jay Haynes, 1876–1905*. Helena, MT: Montana Historical Society Research Center Press, 1983.

Petersen, Gwen. *Yellowstone Pioneers: The Story of Hamilton Stores and Yellowstone National Park*. West Yellowstone, MT: Hamilton Stores, Inc. Oak Tree Publications, 1985.

Reese, Rick. *Greater Yellowstone: The National Park and Adjacent Wildlands*. Helena, MT: Montana Magazine, 1984.

Saunders, Richard L. *Glimpses of Wonderland: The Haynes and Their Postcards of Yellowstone National Park*. Self-published, 1997.

Scofield, Susan C. *The Inn at Old Faithful*. Crowsnest Associates, 1979.

Smith, Phyllis and William Hoy. *The Northern Pacific Railroad & Yellowstone National Park*. Gaithersburg, MD: Keystone Press, 2009.

Watry, Elizabeth A. and Robert V. Goss. *Livingston*. Charleston, SC: Arcadia Publishing, 2009.

Whithorn, Bill and Doris. *Photo History from Yellowstone Park*. Livingston, MT: The Park County News.

Whittlesey, Lee H. and Elizabeth A. Watry. *Yellowstone National Park*. Charleston, SC: Arcadia Publishing, 2008.

Discover Thousands of Local History Books Featuring Millions of Vintage Images

Arcadia Publishing, the leading local history publisher in the United States, is committed to making history accessible and meaningful through publishing books that celebrate and preserve the heritage of America's people and places.

Find more books like this at
www.arcadiapublishing.com

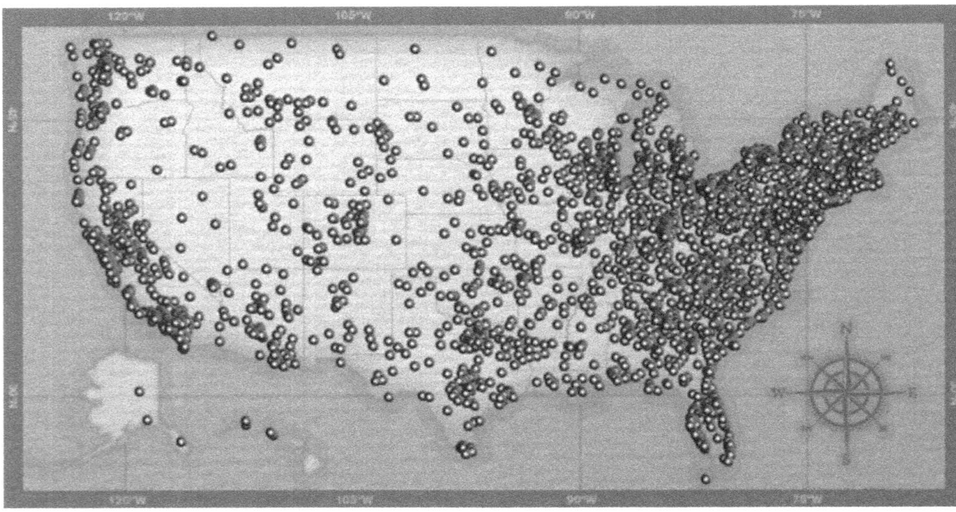

Search for your hometown history, your old stomping grounds, and even your favorite sports team.

Consistent with our mission to preserve history on a local level, this book was printed in South Carolina on American-made paper and manufactured entirely in the United States. Products carrying the accredited Forest Stewardship Council (FSC) label are printed on 100 percent FSC-certified paper.

MADE IN THE USA

www.ingramcontent.com/pod-product-compliance
Lightning Source LLC
LaVergne TN
LVHW070820030926
847199LV00039B/510